RICHARD II

NOTES

including
- *Life of Shakespeare*
- *General Plot Summary*
- *List of Characters*
- *Summaries and Commentaries*
- *Sixteenth-Century Political Theory*
- *Character Summations*
- *Questions for Review*
- *Selected Bibliography*

by
Denis Calandra, Ph.D.
Department of Theater
University of South Florida

INCORPORATED

LINCOLN, NEBRASKA 68501

Editor

Gary Carey, M.A.
University of Colorado

Consulting Editor

James L. Roberts, Ph.D.
Department of English
University of Nebraska

ISBN 0-8220-0068-7
© Copyright 1982
by
C. K. Hillegass
All Rights Reserved
Printed in U.S.A.

1989 Printing

The Cliffs Notes logo, the names "Cliffs" and "Cliffs Notes," and the black and yellow diagonal-stripe cover design are all registered trademarks belonging to Cliffs Notes, Inc., and may not be used in whole or in part without written permission.

Cliffs Notes, Inc.   Lincoln, Nebraska

CONTENTS

RICHARD II NOTES

LIFE OF SHAKESPEARE

Many books have assembled facts, reasonable suppositions, traditions, and speculations concerning the life and career of William Shakespeare. Taken as a whole, these materials give a rather comprehensive picture of England's foremost dramatic poet. Tradition and sober supposition are not necessarily false because they lack proved bases for their existence. It is important, however, that persons interested in Shakespeare should distinguish between *facts* and *beliefs* about his life.

From one point of view, modern scholars are fortunate to know as much as they do about a man of middle-class origin who left a small English country town and embarked on a professional career in sixteenth-century London. From another point of view, they know surprisingly little about the writer who has continued to influence the English language and its drama and poetry for more than three hundred years. Sparse and scattered as these facts of his life are, they are sufficient to prove that a man from Stratford by the name of William Shakespeare wrote the major portion of the thirty-seven plays which scholars ascribe to him. The concise review which follows will concern itself with some of these records.

No one knows the exact date of William Shakespeare's birth. His baptism occurred on Wednesday, April 26, 1564. His father was John Shakespeare, tanner, glover, dealer in grain, and town official of Stratford; his mother, Mary, was the daughter of Robert Arden, a prosperous gentleman-farmer. The Shakespeares lived on Henley Street.

Under a bond dated November 28, 1582, William Shakespeare and Anne Hathaway entered into a marriage contract. The baptism of their eldest child, Susanna, took place in Stratford in May, 1583. One year and nine months later their twins, Hamnet and Judith, were christened in the same church. The parents named them for the poet's friends Hamnet and Judith Sadler.

Early in 1596, William Shakespeare, in his father's name, applied to the College of Heralds for a coat of arms. Although positive proof is lacking, there is reason to believe that the Heralds granted this request, for in 1599 Shakespeare again made application for the right to quarter his coat of arms with that of his mother. Entitled to her father's coat of arms, Mary had lost this privilege when she married John Shakespeare before he held the official status of gentleman.

In May of 1597, Shakespeare purchased New Place, the outstanding residential property in Stratford at that time. Since John Shakespeare had suffered financial reverses prior to this date, William must have achieved success for himself.

Court records show that in 1601 or 1602, William Shakespeare began rooming in the household of Christopher Mountjoy in London. Subsequent disputes between Shakespeare's landlord, Mountjoy, and his son-in-law, Stephen Belott, over Stephen's wedding settlement led to a series of legal actions, and in 1612 the court scribe recorded Shakespeare's deposition of testimony relating to the case.

In July, 1605, William Shakespeare paid four hundred and forty pounds for the lease of a large portion of the tithes on certain real estate in and near Stratford. This was an arrangement whereby Shakespeare purchased half the annual tithes, or taxes, on certain agricultural products from sections of land in and near Stratford. In addition to receiving approximately ten percent income on his investment, he almost doubled his capital. This was possibly the most important and successful investment of his lifetime, and it paid a steady income for many years.

Shakespeare is next mentioned when John Combe, a resident of Stratford, died on July 12, 1614. To his friend, Combe bequeathed the sum of five pounds. These records and similar ones are important, not because of their economic significance but because they prove the existence of a William Shakespeare in Stratford and in London during this period.

On March 25, 1616, William Shakespeare revised his last will and testament. He died on April 23 of the same year. His body lies within the chancel and before the altar of the Stratford church. A rather wry inscription is carved upon his tombstone:

Good Friend, for Jesus' sake, forbear
To dig the dust enclosed here;

> Blest be the man that spares these stones
> And curst be he that moves my bones.

The last direct descendant of William Shakespeare was his granddaughter, Elizabeth Hall, who died in 1670.

These are the most outstanding facts about Shakespeare the man, as apart from those about the dramatist and poet. Such pieces of information, scattered from 1564 through 1616, declare the existence of such a person, not as a writer or actor, but as a private citizen. It is illogical to think that anyone would or could have fabricated these details for the purpose of deceiving later generations.

In similar fashion, the evidence establishing William Shakespeare as the foremost playwright of his day is positive and persuasive. Robert Greene's *Groatsworth of Wit*, in which he attacked Shakespeare, a mere actor, for presuming to write plays in competition with Greene and his fellow playwrights, was entered in the *Stationers' Register* on September 20, 1592. In 1594 Shakespeare acted before Queen Elizabeth, and in 1594 and 1595 his name appeared as one of the shareholders of the Lord Chamberlain's Company. Francis Meres in his *Palladis Tamia* (1598) called Shakespeare "mellifluous and hony-tongued" and compared his comedies and tragedies with those of Plautus and Seneca in excellence.

Shakespeare's continued association with Burbage's company is equally definite. His name appears as one of the owners of the Globe in 1599. On May 19, 1603, he and his fellow actors received a patent from James I designating them as the King's Men and making them Grooms of the Chamber. Late in 1608 or early in 1609, Shakespeare and his colleagues purchased the Blackfriars Theatre and began using it as their winter location when weather made production at the Globe inconvenient.

Other specific allusions to Shakespeare, to his acting and his writing, occur in numerous places. Put together, they form irrefutable testimony that William Shakespeare of Stratford and London was the leader among Elizabethan playwrights.

One of the most impressive of all proofs of Shakespeare's authorship of his plays is the First Folio of 1623, with the dedicatory verse which appeared in it. John Heminge and Henry Condell, members of Shakespeare's own company, stated that they collected and issued the plays as a memorial to their fellow actor. Many contemporary poets contributed eulogies to Shakespeare; one of the best known of these poems is by Ben Jonson, a fellow actor and, later, a friendly rival. Johnson also criticized Shakespeare's dramatic work in *Timber: or, Discoveries* (1641).

Certainly there are many things about Shakespeare's genius and career which the most diligent scholars do not know and cannot explain, but the facts which do exist are sufficient to establish Shakespeare's identity as a man and his authorship of the thirty-seven plays which reputable critics acknowledge to be his.

GENERAL PLOT SUMMARY

The play opens with a dispute between Henry Bolingbroke, Duke of Hereford, and Thomas Mowbray, Duke of Norfolk. Bolingbroke has accused Mowbray of treason, and the two of them exchange insults in the presence of King Richard. After attempts to reconcile them fail, Richard orders them to take part in a traditional chivalric trial by combat. On the field of combat, the king changes his mind and banishes the two men – Bolingbroke for ten years (commuted to six) and Mowbray for life. Then the king makes plans to leave for the wars in Ireland.

Before departing, Richard visits the ailing father of Bolingbroke, John of Gaunt, Duke of Lancaster. Gaunt warns Richard with his dying words that he is flirting with danger and doing great harm to the country by allowing himself to be influenced by his sycophantic courtiers. When he dies, Richard takes possession of all of Gaunt's wealth and leaves for Ireland.

Unhappy with Richard's incompetence as a ruler and worried by his seizure of the Duke of Lancaster's wealth, a number of nobles rally support for Henry Bolingbroke. When Bolingbroke and his army decide to return from exile in France, the rebel forces prepare to confront Richard on his return from Ireland.

The rebel noblemen force the king to abdicate, and Bolingbroke is crowned as Henry IV. Richard is imprisoned in Pomfret Castle, where he faces his death alone, philosophically contemplating the meaning of his fall from grandeur. Sir Pierce of Exton decides solely on his own to execute the deposed king, and then, as a result, he is banished by King Henry. The play ends with Henry IV planning a penitential pilgrimage to the Holy Land.

LIST OF CHARACTERS

King Richard

Historically, he is said to be the handsomest man of his time; in the play, he has great charm and a love for beautiful things. His court is characterized outwardly by its luxury and refinement, but Richard's own particular favorites are greedy men who are interested primarily in the profits made from usurping land, excessive taxation, and fraud. Richard allows himself to be used by these men and, as a result, he is deposed by one of his noblemen whom he sends unfairly into exile.

Bolingbroke

Henry, Duke of Hereford and Lancaster; he takes revenge on Richard after the king unfairly banishes him from England and, moreover, claims all of Henry's family lands and wealth after Henry's father, John of Gaunt, dies. Bolingbroke is a "model" Englishman and, for that reason, he is not entirely convinced that he has the right to usurp the crown from a man who *seems* corrupt even though he is supposed to be God's deputy on earth.

York

He is Richard's most powerful supporter, and when Richard leaves with his forces to fight in Ireland, he leaves York in charge of England. York is honest and good throughout the play and because of these qualities, he finally cannot condone Richard's unprincipled actions; thus he changes his allegiance to Bolingbroke and his supporters.

Aumerle

York's headstrong son remains loyal to Richard throughout the play, despite the fact that this loyalty threatens his relationship with his father. He even becomes involved in a plot to assassinate Bolingbroke, but at the pleading of his mother, he confesses his deed and is pardoned by Bolingbroke.

Queen Isabella

She appears four times in the play and, each time, she is characterized by her gentleness and her devotion to Richard. Moreover, there is a feeling of helplessness about her. Her grief becomes despair when she realizes that her husband has been deposed. She tries, however, to goad him into at least a *show* of valor and resistance when she speaks with him on his way to prison.

Mowbray

Clearly, he had a hand in the murder of Gloucester, even though he denies it. Richard exiles him for life, probably in order to remove this hand-chosen assassin from the country. Mowbray dies abroad, during one of the Crusades.

Northumberland

A powerful and aggressive character; his allegiance is early aligned with Bolingbroke. He fights alongside Bolingbroke and arranges for Richard's surrender. It is he who breaks up the last of Richard's conspirators.

Percy

Northumberland's son. He is an eager soldier, chivalrous, and an active supporter of Bolingbroke.

Duchess of Gloucester

It was the murder of her husband which caused Bolingbroke to accuse Mowbray of assassination and treason. She begs old Gaunt to take revenge on Richard; her anger is fiery and passionate. She dies of grief for her husband.

Duchess of York

Her loyalty is, foremost, to her son, who is loyal to Richard. Her whole character revolves around Aumerle's safety. She herself is fearless before Bolingbroke, but she fears the latter's power to silence her son's seemingly treasonous words and deeds.

Surrey

He is sympathetic with Aumerle and refutes Fitzwater's claim that Aumerle, in Fitzwater's presence, did take credit for Gloucester's death.

Carlisle

He is ever-loyal to Richard because he sees Richard's role as one that was heaven-ordained. He rails against Bolingbroke but, importantly, he also chides Richard for the kind of king he has been. In the end, Bolingbroke pardons him because of his unusually high character.

Abbot of Westminster

He hears Aumerle's wish to revenge himself on Bolingbroke and, therefore, he invites Aumerle home so that the two of them can make further plans.

Ross and Willoughby

Representatives of the followers of Bolingbroke.

Fitzwater

He swears that he heard Aumerle take full credit for Gloucester's murder. Surrey takes issue with this statement, and Fitzwater challenges him to a duel.

Exton

Believing that Bolingbroke wishes him to kill Richard, he does so; immediately afterward, however, he is sure that he acted rashly. Bolingbroke banishes him.

Salisbury

Richard leaves him in charge of the military forces while he fights in Ireland. He is upset when he discovers that he has no Welsh support for Richard when he knows that Bolingbroke and his supporters are ready to attack Richard.

Scroop

He announces to Richard that the common people have championed Bolingbroke as their favorite. He appears only in Act III, Scenes 2 and 3.

Berkeley

In charge of the troops guarding Bristol Castle, he is rebuked when Bolingbroke confronts him, and he refers to Bolingbroke as Hereford—and not as Lancaster.

Bushy and Green

They are followers of Richard, but they are neither heroic nor staunch in their loyalty. They plot, connive, and flee at the approach of danger. Bolingbroke corners them finally and has them killed. They are representative of the low-class of flatterers whom Richard surrounds himself with.

Bagot

He has a part only slightly larger than Bushy and Green; otherwise, he is not distinguishable from them.

SUMMARIES AND COMMENTARIES

ACT I – SCENE I

Summary

King Richard II opens the play by asking old John of Gaunt if he has brought John's son, Henry Bolingbroke, to substantiate charges of treason which he has made against Thomas Mowbray, Duke of Norfolk. After asking Gaunt if he has already questioned his son on the matter, Richard asks that the two men be brought before him; Richard greets them formally, and then he asks Henry Bolingbroke to clarify his case against Mowbray. Bolingbroke charges Mowbray with being a "traitor and a miscreant," but before he can finish speaking, Mowbray breaks in and offers a counter-accusation: "I do defy him and I spit at him,/ Call him a slanderous coward and a villain." Mowbray suggests that they settle their quarrel by dueling at Coventry, and Bolingbroke throws down his glove as a symbol of his counter-challenge, according to the rites of knighthood. After Mowbray retrieves the glove and accepts the challenge, the king asks Bolingbroke to explain his accusation against Mowbray. Bolingbroke levels the charges: "All the treasons of these eighteen years" have their origin in Mowbray; he did plot the murder of the Duke of Gloucester. Mowbray responds that he committed *one* grave sin in the past – laying an ambush for old Gaunt's life, but he has since repented it. He denies killing Gloucester. The king tries to calm them both with the words "Forget, forgive; conclude and be agreed," and he appeals to old Gaunt for help in the matter. Gaunt cannot decide what to do, and so he exits. Meanwhile, Mowbray refuses to withdraw the challenge. "The purest treasure," he says, which "mortal times afford/ Is spotless reputation. . . ." Therefore, he tells Richard, the king can command his life, but not his shame; Bolingbroke's reply is similar: "Shall I seem crestfallen in my father's sight?" Richard seemingly cannot determine which of the men is lying and, therefore, he refuses to arbitrate any longer; he orders that the duel shall take place at Coventry on Saint Lambert's Day (September 17): "There shall your swords and lances arbitrate."

Commentary

As is the case with Shakespeare's other history plays, this play has as its central concern a civil strife which threatens a country with a weak government. Thus, *Richard II* opens with a scene that graphically illustrates the point: two nobles are locked in bitter argument over who is most loyal to the crown, and the only logical outcome would seem to be a physical struggle, even to the death. The best that the king can do is agree to let them fight.

The character of old Gaunt is important here because he is referred to several times as an "old" man and is therefore supposed to be a "sage" man. Richard appeals to Gaunt to help settle the argument, but with no success; neither the ruler nor he who possesses the wisdom of age can calm the troubled waters in this first scene; only a decision based on formal violence will decide the issue.

Note in particular the chivalric atmosphere of this scene. When the challengers speak to the king and to each other, they use a very formal style of address. For example, Bolingbroke first speaks to his king:

> In the devotion of a subject's love,
> Tend'ring the precious safety of my prince,
> And free from other misbegotten hate,
> Come I appellant to this princely presence.

(31-34)

And Mowbray, when he accepts the challenge, also speaks in a formal manner:

> I take it up; and by that sword I swear
> Which gently laid my knighthood on my shoulder,
> I'll answer then in any fair degree
> Or chivalrous design of knightly trial.

(78-81)

The formal speech patterns and the chivalric code of behavior here act as metaphors for order and control. These men are preparing to kill each other, but they are going about it in a gentlemanly way. Such formal patterns exist, according to Shakespeare's orthodox belief, in the world of government too. There is always an attempt — even when it becomes a struggle — to keep the most violent passions regulated within a pattern.

Speaking of formal patterns, we must not ignore the real passion and invective in some of the remarks which the opponents hurl at each other. Take, for example, Bolingbroke's promise to tear out his own tongue and "spit it bleeding" in Mowbray's face rather than withdraw from the fight. This is naked, unbridled passion. But it is spoken within the formal context of a verbal tournament, preluding the tournament at Coventry. And, in reference to passion, there is an important, implicit clue as to the murderer of Gloucester in this scene. Mowbray has indeed had a hand in killing him (and that's what Bolingbroke accuses him of), but Mowbray did it at Richard's request. When Bolingbroke utters the words, "the death," Mowbray says, "I slew him not; but, to my own disgrace/ Neglected my *sworn duty* in that case" (italics mine). Mowbray swore, without a doubt, to Richard to see to it that Gloucester was either killed by his hand or by Mowbray's order.

One more matter that should not be neglected in any discussion of language in this scene includes the fact that the language, besides being mostly chivalrous and formal, suggests a religious theme in several places: such words as "miscreant," "innocent souls," "rites of knighthood," and "our sacred blood" occur frequently. This language will be of even more importance later in the play.

ACT I – SCENE 2

Summary

The scene takes place at the London palace of John of Gaunt; old Gaunt is talking to the Duchess of Gloucester, who is paying him a visit. The duchess is very upset; she wants revenge and she hopes that old Gaunt will see to it that revenge is exacted because Gloucester, her husband, was Gaunt's brother. Gaunt advises his sister-in-law that they can't do anything against the "butchers of [Gloucester's] life." They had best leave the "quarrel to the will of Heaven." The duchess is shocked at Gaunt's apparent lack of will to take vengeance for her "dear lord." Her husband's blood was Gaunt's own blood, she emphasizes. Likewise, she tells Gaunt that her murdered husband and Gaunt shared the same womb, but Gaunt refuses to submit to her tactics. The duchess, however, continues; she argues that "to safeguard thine own life/ The best way is to venge my Gloucester's death." Gaunt explains that his hands are tied; the king, "God's deputy," caused the murder, hence revenge must be left to heaven. One cannot defy God's appointed deputy in England, he insists. The duchess appears to acquiesce and bids Gaunt goodbye. She hopes that at least right will triumph when Bolingbroke and Mowbray fight at Coventry, and that Bolingbroke's spear "may enter butcher Mowbray's breast!" Weeping, she bids Gaunt farewell.

Commentary

Shakespeare's plays were written for performance without any breaks between the scenes or the acts. The flow of the scenes, their placement, and the effect which was created by contrasting elements in the scene constitutes his chief technical resource. In the first scene, for example, Richard tries to arbitrate a dispute between two peers of his realm. The issue is one of state—loyalty to the king—and also a personal matter of honor between two men of arms. The tone of the opening scene tells us that something is *wrong* in the state of England. Scene 2, appropriately, personalizes this *wrongness*, this grief, by showing us a woman lamenting aloud both the loss of her husband *and* the fact that she is likely not to see proper vengeance done. That she is suffering personally is certain, and her confusion is clear in her last speech, for she finds it difficult to say farewell to old Gaunt.

> Commend me to thy brother, Edmund York.
> Lo! this is all: nay, yet depart not so;
> Though this be all, do not so quickly go.
> I shall remember more. Bid him . . . Ah! What?
> With all good speed at Plashy visit me.
>
> (62-65)

The phrasing—"Lo! . . . nay, yet depart not. . . . Bid him . . . Ah! What?"—tells more about her distraught state of mind than the words themselves.

At the beginnings of the scene, when the duchess tries to play on Gaunt's feelings for his murdered brother, her language echoes Christian and biblical phrases. She refers to the patriarch:

> Edward's seven sons, whereof thyself art one,
> Were as seven vials of his sacred blood,
> Or seven fair branches springing from one root.
>
> (11-13)

As she continues, her emotion wells up.

> But Thomas, my dear lord, my life, my Gloucester,
> One vial full of Edward's sacred blood, ...

> . . . is hacked down . . .
> Ah! Gaunt, his blood was thine!
>
> (16-22)

The effect of this speech is to reinforce her feelings of loss by emphasizing the "sacredness" of their common father's blood. The irony, and a serious religious and political problem for Shakespeare's age, is that another father-figure, one who is also "sacred," is Richard II, the king, and he has had a hand in perpetrating the crime. Gaunt has relatively few lines in this scene, and for good reason. He, like others around him, feels impotent before this impossible dilemma. This old and sage Gaunt, in his helplessness in the face of personal and public grief, is an important early theatrical image in the play. He can only lamely repeat the formula:

> God's is the quarrel; for God's substitute,
> His deputy anointed in His sight,
> Hath caused his death. . . .
>
> (37-39)

ACT I – SCENE 3

Summary

Richard and his knights arrive at Coventry, on a field prepared for single combat, and enter to the sound of trumpets. Then Mowbray enters with a herald. The king bids the Marshal to "demand of yonder champion" the cause of the present quarrel. After Mowbray is asked the cause of his being here, he repeats his case, promising to prove himself true and, furthermore, promising to prove Bolingbroke "a traitor to my God, my King, and me." Trumpets are heard again, and Bolingbroke, armed like his counterpart, enters the scene. Richard asks the Marshal once again to inquire the cause of complaint. The Marshal does so, and Bolingbroke repeats his previous accusation: Mowbray is a traitor, "foul and dangerous." Bolingbroke then asks permission to bid farewell to the king by kissing his ring. The king acknowledges the request and descends from his seat to "fold him in our arms." Richard states that despite whose blood will be shed, no revenge will be taken.

Bolingbroke then takes leave of the king, his kinsmen, his followers, and finally his father. He bids them to shed no tears and promises to perform valiantly for his father's sake. His father, in turn, bids him to "be swift like lightning" in the fight.

Mowbray then has his turn to bid farewell to the king, claiming to be a "loyal, just, and upright gentleman" who will fight without boasting about it. "As gentle and as jocund as to jest/ Go I to fight," he says, for "truth hath a quiet breast."

Before the fight begins, however, King Richard throws his baton to the ground as a signal to halt the proceedings. "Let them lay by their helmets and their spears," he says "and both return to their chairs again." Richard explains that he does not wish to see blood spilled by his countrymen, as in civil war, and therefore will banish the two contestants from England. Bolingbroke is not to return for ten years, while Mowbray is banished for life. The two men accept their sentences gracefully, though Mowbray, who is never to return, expresses a deep sadness that he will not be able to speak the English language again; he feels condemned to a "speechless death."

As the two turn to leave, Richard stops them and makes them lay their hands on his royal sword and promise never to come into contact with one another again nor to engage in any treasonous act; never are they "to plot, contrive, or complot any ill." Both swear accordingly, but Bolingbroke has a parting word with Mowbray; he asks him—now that he is banished and free from other punishment—to confess the crime against the state which he has committed. Mowbray replies that he'd rather be "from heaven banished" than admit to such a thing. He exits then.

Richard turns to Gaunt and immediately reduces old Gaunt's son's sentence from ten years to six years because Gaunt's old eyes betray a "grieved heart." Bolingbroke gratefully accepts the commutation of his sentence and muses on the ease with which Richard can change the course of another man's life: "Such is the breath of kings." Gaunt also thanks the king, but remains saddened because he is an old man who may not live the six years before his son returns. When the king cheerfully reminds him that he is in good health and will live many more years, Gaunt stops him short by saying that even the king "cannot buy my breath." The king questions Gaunt, wondering why he did not defend his son more vehemently. Gaunt replies that he was urged to speak as a judge and not to argue "like a father." His duty to the judgment process forced him to remain as objective as possible, and now he must suffer privately for it.

In the last minutes of the scene, Bolingbroke and his father take leave of each other. Gaunt tries to cheer up his son by saying that it won't be too long before he returns and that if he keeps his mind on other things, the time of exile will pass quickly. Bolingbroke, however asks:

> . . . who can hold a fire in his hand
> By thinking on the frosty Caucasus?
> Or cloy the hungry edge of appetite
> By bare imagination of a feast?
> Or wallow naked in December snow
> By thinking on fantastic summer's heat?
>
> (294-99)

He departs, swearing that wherever he wanders he can at least boast that "though banished, [he is] yet a trueborn Englishman."

Commentary

Notice the progression of this scene. It begins as a highly formal, almost ritualistic display in the chivalric tradition. The accused and the accusing parties are announced; they state their cases, make their farewells, and prepare to fight. It ends with a father and a son, Gaunt and Bolingbroke, saying goodbye for six years, or, considering Gaunt's age, maybe for the last time in their lives. The scene moves from the affairs of state in a public ceremony to the intimate details of personal, familial relationships. That very pattern, you will recall, was the pattern of scenes one and two. Here it is repeated, with continuous focus on the principals in the drama.

When Richard pronounces the words "orderly proceed" at the start of the scene, he is, of course, sounding the keynote to all of Shakespeare's history plays again. The ritual of this hand-to-hand combat, though it is enacted to resolve a passionate dispute and may end in bloodshed, will be carried out according to mutually acknowledged rules. One must imagine the start of this scene as being filled with suggestions of the spectacle of a medieval tournament. Representatives of the opposing camps march in, present themselves to the king, speak their pieces, and take up positions on an elaborate stage tableau. The picture on stage and the accompanying regular trumpet blasts are clear metaphors for a kind of *order*. And at the center of this ordered world is, of course, King Richard, who is stationed upstage to observe the proceedings. When he descends from his raised platform (which was traditional) and walks downstage to stop the proceedings later in the scene, he travels quite a distance (the depth of Shakespeare's stage was about 25 feet), reinforcing his pivotal place on the stage and in the political picture.

The language of Bolingbroke, describing himself and Mowbray as two men who "vow [to take] a long and weary pilgrimage," continues the religious imagery which is germane to the subject of this play. Bolingbroke wants to take a long farewell with his father because it may be their last farewell. But before he launches into his private farewell, he is embraced by the king, a poignant moment when one considers the scene later in the play when the two of them meet again—when Richard renounces his throne to Bolingbroke. Richard hands him the crown then. Here, the father of the nation, as it were, embraces one of his "sons"; later, that "son" will depose him. Bolingbroke bids farewell to his faithful followers, then to his actual father, Gaunt.

Notice, too, the way that Shakespeare contrasts the characters of these opponents by suggesting a difference in their bearing in these scenes. When they first encountered one another in the first scene of this act, Mowbray made a point of contrasting his own response to the situation with Bolingbroke's. Implicitly, he is claiming that Bolingbroke is somewhat hot-headed and, therefore, less creditable than himself. There he said:

> Let not my cold words here accuse my zeal.
> 'Tis not the trial of a woman's war,
> The bitter clamour of two eager tongues,
> Can arbitrate this cause betwixt us twain;
> The blood is hot that must be cooled for this.
>
> (I.i.47-51)

He has apparently listened to Bolingbroke's enraged words and has decided to respond with a posture of perfect reasonableness. In this scene, he strikes the same theme when he says, "Truth hath a quiet breast." The reason for this relatively calm bearing might be his quiet confidence that the king is on his side and, therefore, he shall come to no harm. Whatever the reason, the posture of one combatant being more feverish than the other is important for dramatic reasons. Besides adding variety in characterization, this contrast prepares for a similar contrast later during the deposition scene (IV.i). Notice there how quietly Bolingbroke endures the lengthy diatribes of King Richard II.

An important dramatic facet in this scene is Richard's decision to stop the combat and to exile the opponents. All of the spectacle and verbal exchange in the scene is leading up to a violent combat which never takes place. Why does Shakespeare have Richard stop the fight? For one thing, Richard is, in fact, indebted to Mowbray for being instrumental in eliminating a potential enemy (Gloucester). For another, to allow the combat to go forward and risk the life of the apparently popular Bolingbroke would be a poor political move. It seems best to appear the wise and kind ruler by preventing any civil bloodshed at all. Notice that Richard also manages to banish Mowbray, the one who has evidence against him, for life, while commuting the sentence of Bolingbroke from ten years to six years, further mollifying his potential political opponents. Rulers in Shakespeare's age would have been familiar with Machiavelli's famous *Prince*, a popular and rather cynical manual for rulers, and would have known that it is always wiser to appear harsher at first, making severe punishments all at once, and then to soften one's stance with mercy. The mercy, however, is not received quite as Richard had expected, and this irritates him.

There is a serious undertone of antagonism between Richard, on the one hand, and Gaunt and his son, on the other. Richard knows very well what he is doing in commuting the sentence as he does, and he is hoping that Gaunt will receive this lordly gesture appropriately. When Gaunt takes up his son's cue on the words "such is the breath of kings" and tells the king that though he can easily send a man into exile or even cut a man's life short, he *still* does not have the power to add one minute to a man's life, he is raising a very sensitive issue and one very important to a central theme of this play. In a play in which the deposition of God's appointed minister, the king, is a central action, it is a highly charged dramatic moment when the matter of the limitation of the power of the king is raised. None of this by-play is openly acknowledged by the speakers, but their words are certainly spoken with an awareness of all connotations. What Gaunt is saying, in effect, is that although Richard may be God's anointed and appointed deputy, he is certainly *not* God Himself. One wonders if the conversation which he had with his sister-in-law in the previous scene, coupled with the present sorrow of saying goodbye to his son, has given him some of the courage which the Duchess of Gloucester found wanting. That Gaunt's remarks have the desired effect on Richard is clear from the way in which the king exits, with two clipped lines reiterating the sentence just meted out:

> Cousin, farewell, and uncle bid him so;
> Six years we banish him, and he shall go.
>
> (247-48)

The last moments of the scene are especially important for their emotional tone. There is speed in the delivery of the lines between Gaunt and his son, Bolingbroke, that belies the feelings underneath. Bolingbroke is silent at first, until his father urges him to speak.

> *Gaunt*:   O, to what purpose dost thou hoard thy words,
>   That thou return'st no greeting to thy friends?
> *Bolingbroke*:   I have too few to take my leave of you,
>   When the tongue's office should be prodigal
>   To breathe the abundant dolour of the heart.
> *Gaunt*:   Thy grief is but thy absence for a time.
> *Bolingbroke*:   Joy absent, grief is present for that time.
> *Gaunt*:   What is six winters? They are quickly gone.
> *Bolingbroke*:   To men in joy; but grief makes one hour ten.
> *Gaunt*:   Call it a travel that thou tak'st for pleasure.
>
> (255-64)

This seems a very genuine scene, psychologically. Gaunt's distress is shown by the fact that he is using "arguments" to make his son feel better, which he had, just a few minutes before, rebuked the king for using—that is, that the exile really won't be so long, that it really is only a temporary absence. In addition, it is as if the rush of words they exchange is a way of covering up feelings they would rather not have to cope with. There is an irony in the remark which Gaunt makes to his son, telling him that his absence will serve as a foil to his coming home, and make the coming home that much more joyous. In a way, this is true, for Bolingbroke's return will eventually lead to his becoming king, albeit reluctantly. His return *will* seem greater because of the absence. Also, Richard's behavior, by comparison, will make Bolingbroke seem greater. Interestingly, this metaphor of a *foil* carries on into the *Henry IV* plays. There, we find Bolingbroke an older and a wearier man, now the king himself, having to deal with a recalcitrant son, Prince Hal. Throughout the play, Hal's escapades with the lower orders of society are described in such a way that they can be seen as setting his "true" (princely) self off as a jewel is set off by the less precious metal leaf which serves as backing for it in a setting.

There is superb humaneness in old Gaunt as he gives his son some conventional fatherly advice at the end of the scene. He is trying to be perfectly reasonable and allay his son's fears: don't think that the king has banished you, but rather think that you have banished the king; try to think that a foul pestilence sits in the land and you are better off out of the country. In a sense, there *is* a truth in this, in that there is a less than perfect king on the throne, but Bolingbroke can answer only from his heart, and none of his father's arguments make him feel any better. Who can "wallow naked in December snow/ By thinking on fantastic summer's heat?" he asks. The reality of banishment will be so painful that he won't be able to delude himself for a minute into believing otherwise. At the very last, however, Bolingbroke exits with an important, manly, and patriotic flourish:

> Where'er I wander, boast of this I can,
> Though banish'd, yet a trueborn Englishman.
>
> (308-9)

These, undoubtedly, are the words of a hero.

ACT I–SCENE 4

Summary

The scene opens shortly after the last. Richard is subtly trying to test the loyalty of Aumerle, the son of the Duke of York, and, at the same time, to find out from him what Bolingbroke said on his departure, for Aumerle escorted Bolingbroke away. Aumerle says that Bolingbroke said only "Farewell." Clearly, he does not like Bolingbroke and did not enjoy escorting him away, feigning feelings of fond farewell. Richard does not want to seem villainous, and so he reminds Aumerle that Bolingbroke is "our cousin." He then explores another avenue of conversation; he says that he has had certain of his men — Bushy, Bagot, and Green — observing the country people, and they report that the banished Bolingbroke is popular among the commoners. He ponders,

> How he did seem to dive into their hearts
> With humble and familiar courtesy,
> What reverence he did throw away on slaves,
> Wooing poor craftsmen with the craft of smiles. . . .
>
> (25-28)

To Richard, it seems "as were our England in reversion his."

Green then speaks up and reminds Richard that, at least, Bolingbroke is out of the way; now they must turn their attention to the pressing problem of the Irish rebellion. Richard decides to go into battle himself against the rebels, and he plans to do so with the greatest assurance of success. To that end, he decides that he must first fill his coffers with riches borrowed from (and demanded from) his country's nobles. At that point, Bushy rushes in with the news that Gaunt is extremely ill, probably dying. Richard wishes the old man "good speed" (to death). In fact, his comment is quite mercenary:

> The lining of his coffers shall make coats
> To deck our soldiers for these Irish wars.
>
> (61-62)

They all exit then to go to Gaunt's bedside.

Commentary

Here we see Richard in close-ups; he is a man who is accustomed to exploiting his countrymen, and in this scene he is a marked contrast to the "true-born Englishman" who bade us farewell in the previous scene. Not only does Shakespeare show Richard quite openly preparing to take his country's wealth to spend on a foreign war, but also hoping for an early death for the venerable old Gaunt. This is rather bold characterization, somewhat melodramatic, and more typical of Shakespeare's early plays than his later ones. There is no question at this point where an audience's sympathies lie.

Note also the character of Aumerle in this scene. He is a young man, the son of the Duke of York, and naturally enough he shows loyalty to his king. He is proud of having successfully feigned grief at Bolingbroke's departure, and he happily joins Bagot and Green at the king's side. Shakespeare will later sound this note of feigned grief when Richard gives up the crown. There, it will be Bolingbroke who sarcastically commends Richard for putting on a good show of suffering. The matter of loyalty to the king is important, with regard to Aumerle, because of his actions later in the play when he is chided by his father for behavior disloyal to the new king, Bolingbroke. In the end, of course, Bolingbroke pardons Aumerle, but that pardon will seem all the more magnanimous because of the memory of this early scene in which Aumerle is quite clearly a loyal ally of Richard's and a foe of Bolingbroke's.

Consider the dramatic effect when Richard sarcastically bids his followers to come with him to the dying Gaunt's bedside: "Come, gentlemen, let's all go visit him;/ Pray God we may make haste and come too late!" And they reply, to a man: "Amen!" The contrast with the closing of the previous scene is a powerful one.

ACT II – SCENE 1

Summary

This scene takes place at Ely House in London, where Gaunt lies ill. His first speech forms a sort of "bridge" between the end of the last scene and this act. Speaking to his brother, the Duke of York, Gaunt asks, "Will the king come that I may breathe my last/ In wholesome counsel to his unstaid youth?" Clearly, Gaunt is worried about conditions in England. York, however, has no easy words of consolation; he thinks that the king is beyond listening ("all in vain comes counsel to his ear"); he thinks that the king listens only to young men who are more concerned with aping Continental fashions than coping with England's political troubles. Still, however, Gaunt hopes that his advice won't be wasted. He reasons that dying men are listened to more carefully because it is recognized that their words are precious because they are so scarce.

Acknowledging that he probably sounds like an Old Testament prophet, Gaunt charges Richard with the sin of wasting himself in a "rash fierce blaze of riot" which "cannot last." He is determined to convert the erring Richard to a better life worthy of his role as king. He appeals strongly to the patriotic sentiments of the audience as he rhetorically describes England:

> This royal throne of kings, this sceptred isle,
> This earth of majesty, this seat of Mars,
> This other Eden, demi-paradise. . . .
>
> (40-42)

Then Gaunt reverses the imagery and speaks of the shame which has been brought to England of late, how Richard turned this paradise into a shameful place and turned this fortress-like isle into a prison. As the king enters, York hastily warns Gaunt to temper his rage, saying that "young hot colts being raged do rage the more."

Richard, with his favorite courtiers, approaches Gaunt and is amazed at the old man's invective. Gaunt charges that Richard is the sicker of the two men, and he extends the idea of sickness and infection to include England itself: "Thy deathbed," he says, "is no lesser than thy land,/ Wherein thou liest in reputation sick. . . ." He points to the covey of political sycophants which the king surrounds himself with; the crown of England cannot encompass all these "thousand flatterers," Gaunt warns. Richard is no king; Richard is no more than a greedy landlord to his country.

Richard loses his composure and abruptly stops the old man: if Gaunt were not the brother to great Edward's son, he would soon have his head separated from his body. Gaunt is not impressed. He reminds the company that that sort of scruple didn't bother Richard when he ended Gloucester's life. As Gaunt is taken out, he turns and hopes that "these words hereafter thy tormentors be!"

Gaunt's death is announced shortly thereafter by Northumberland, and the Duke of York is distressed to hear Richard almost gloat over "the plate, coin, revenues, and moveables . . ." of old Gaunt. What is to become of the entire system of allegiance and inheritance, he asks, if Richard can so capriciously take the lands and property of Gaunt, which rightfully belong to Gaunt's son, Bolingbroke? If Richard does this, York warns him that he "plucks a thousand dangers on [his] head." Richard is unmoved; he means to immediately "seize into our hands/ His plate, his goods, his money, and his lands," and to that end he orders Bushy to arrange the transfer of possessions.

When the king is gone, Northumberland, Willoughby, and Ross discuss the state of the nation. Northumberland fears that banishment will be the punishment if one of Richard's flatterers chooses to decide to denounce him. Ross points to the grievous, unjust taxes now levied on commoners and nobles alike, and Willoughby mentions the plethora of "blank checks" and "forced loans." The three men see no hope for England; ". . . unavoided is the danger now." The times demand revolt, and Ross urges Northumberland to lead the revolt. Northumberland then gives them the news that already he has had news from Bolingbroke; Gaunt's son has gathered a large number of highly placed sympathizers who have ships and some "three thousand men." As soon as Richard leaves for Ireland, Bolingbroke means to fight to reclaim what is his. Moreover, Northumberland promises them that they personally will soon have a chance to "redeem . . . the blemished crown,/ Wipe off the dust that hides our sceptre's gilt,/ And make high majesty look like itself."

Commentary

This long scene begins with the individual rage of an esteemed old man who is soon to breathe his last, and it ends with the suggestion that the rage has spread to large numbers of people who are prepared to do something about it. The situation is a potentially revolutionary one, and Shakespeare traces the development of political turmoil by first allowing one man to speak his frustration and bear the insults of a capricious ruler, and then showing the effect of this scene of humiliation on those who have witnessed it. When Northumberland, Ross, and Willoughby conspire at the very end of the scene to join forces with the rebellious army of Bolingbroke, we have a feeling that there is a rightness to their decision. We not only hear *about* Richard's ill-treatment of deserving countrymen, but we witness that ill-treatment. Shakespeare's dramatic strategy is at its most effective here.

In the first conversation between York and Gaunt, Gaunt is perhaps a symbol for the sickly state of the nation, for there is the suggestion that what is symbolically best about the nation is languishing at the moment. Then after York prepares the ground with references to corrupt foreign influences and herds of flatterers, it is Gaunt who delivers the rousing patriotic speech which is the emotional center of the entire scene. By the end of the speech, it is as though Gaunt is identified with all that is good and noble and blessed about England. The scene gains further dramatic significance by the fact that these are the words of a dying man. Point for point, the features of England which Gaunt mentions in his rousing speech are those features which are being misshapen by the actions of the king and his court. "This seat of Mars" — England — a proud, warring nation, we are soon to learn, has become so craven that it gains more and spends more from its cleverly concluded truces than it does from the actual spoils of war. And when Northumberland and his friends speak at the end of the scene, it is clear that they *loath* the new set of priorities that Richard has set for the nation. Even the war fought in Ireland is fought on borrowed, extorted, and stolen money, and it is fought for a purely *imperialistic* purpose — that is, to fill the coffers of the profligate king. Gaunt's charges are keen and forceful: "This fortress built by nature for herself," "this precious stone set in the silver sea" has become instead a prison "bound in with shame" and an object to be pawned, "now leased out." Gaunt is responding to the corruption of his England in the interests of the private indulgence of a bad king, and Shakespeare, for his part, like many of his contemporaries, is here making unhappy reference to changes in the economic system which was taking place in Elizabethan England. The new order for England would be the order of a profit-oriented world. Shakespeare also sounds the religious note of the play anew in this scene when he makes reference to the "Christian service and true chivalry" of the former "royal kings" of England. At the end of Gaunt's speech, one can imagine the old man being somewhat exhausted, especially when he utters the lines,

> Ah! would the scandal vanish with my life,
> How happy then were my ensuing death!

(67-68)

His own strength is diminishing in strong contrast with the swift and lively entry of Richard and his queen and courtiers. Richard, true to his reputation, always travels "in style," as it were. Whenever he comes onto the scene, it is always with a verbal flourish and an entourage. He is a man who likes "entrances," a man with a special penchant for acting. Consider the situation when Gaunt utters his last tired breath at the end of his patriotic tirade, and Richard bursts onto the scene. Notice the way in which Richard speaks to the old man. His speech is short and clipped, and his treatment of Gaunt is disrespectful, to say the least. First, there is the exchange between them on the subject of Gaunt's punning comment on the state of his health and the meaning of his name – gaunt, sickly, and thin. Richard's words are, at first, questions, one after the other – "What comfort, man? How is it with aged Gaunt?"; "Can sick men play so nicely with their names?"; "Should dying men flatter . . . those that live?" But when Gaunt loses patience, as an old man deprived of the comfort of having a son near him as he himself nears death, he launches a direct attack on the king and his court. The king, in turn, responds viciously. Gaunt's reference to the "thousand flatterers [who] sit within thy crown" and more specifically to the fact that Richard is dangerously close to deposing himself strikes a raw nerve within Richard. Earlier, he entered the scene self-assured and confident that Gaunt was no threat to him because of his illness; he has come to Ely House in the first place to collect the old man's wealth, but now he loses his composure at these words and suddenly attacks the old man:

> A lunatic, lean-witted fool,
> Presuming on an ague's privilege,
> Dar'st with thy frozen admonition
> Make pale our cheek, chasing the royal blood
> With fury from his native residence.
>
> (115-19)

This attack adds cowardice and foolhardiness to the list of Richard's faults. One should remember, however, that Richard's response to any attack on himself is, in orthodox terms, justified; he *is* the king and, therefore, an entity apart from ordinary mortals. The complication in this scene, and indeed in the play as a whole, is that this king seems unworthy of the divine office he occupies. His attacker, old Gaunt, especially after the emotional "this other Eden" speech, is much more the "kingly" figure to be identified with England's virtues than the actual king himself.

Before Gaunt exits, he virtually accuses the king of the murder of Gloucester, and he warns him that these words will later haunt him:

> Live in thy shame, but die not shame with thee!
> These words hereafter thy tormentors be!
>
> (135-36)

The words will haunt him, and we should recall them when we witness the last scenes of the play, when the king faces death and despondency—as old Gaunt now does.

One reason for Shakespeare's writing the next part of the scene, between Richard and York, is that it offers a point of contrast between the two "old" men (York and Gaunt) in their responses to the king. We have already witnessed the conversation between York and Gaunt, and we know that York is unhappy with the state of England, though he is less likely to become infuriated and risk any treasonous act or statement. He tried to conciliate old Gaunt, tried to calm him in the face of the king, and now he uses the words of a diplomat to quell the king's anger toward Gaunt:

> I do beseech your Majesty, impute his words
> To wayward sickliness and age in him. . . .
>
> (141-42)

York has a careful nature here; clearly, he knows just how explosive the situation is and doesn't want anyone to risk upsetting whatever equilibrium prevails. He will retain this role throughout the entire play, even after the rebels prove successful in deposing Richard.

It is significant that this "normative" figure, York, has his patience tried when Gaunt's death is announced, and the king, without the least trace of remorse, makes plans to immediately collect the booty he came for in the first place. The king's words, ironically, point to his own future situation: "The ripest fruit first falls, and so doth he;/ His time is spent, our pilgrimage must be. So much for that" (153-55). The king himself is "ripest" in the sense that he is most near-ly "rotten"; and the king will indeed follow Gaunt on a "pilgrim-age"—to humiliation and death. Richard breaks off these thoughts in mid-sentence and turns his mind to Gaunt's "plate, coins, and revenues." It is here that York approaches exasperation: "How long shall I be patient?" he asks and begins a lengthy discourse on the falseness of Richard's conduct. One must imagine Richard's de-meanor through all this long speech of York's. His interrupting words are: "Why, uncle, what's the matter?" The tone is almost cer-tainly sarcastic because it couldn't fail to be clear to anyone exactly *what* the matter *is*. York continues his desperate argument, com-pletely unaware that, at best, the king is merely tolerating his words. York concludes his argument about succession: since Richard is violating rights of inheritance and succession by seizing Gaunt's goods, he is putting the very idea of succession in jeopardy:

> Take Hereford's rights away, and take from Time
> His charters and his customary rights;
> Let not tomorrow then ensue today;
> Be not thyself.

> (195-98)

Indeed, in being a bad king, Richard is *not* being himself, kingship being by definition divine and therefore good. Richard is totally un-moved by this speech and, single-mindedly, he repeats his inten-tions:

> Think what you will, we seize into our hands
> His plate, his goods, his money, and his lands.

> (209-10)

York departs in despair, a mood which will change to hope in the rebellious persons of Northumberland, Willoughby, and Ross.

Remember that these three men have been present for most of the foregoing scene and have witnessed the behavior of the king—both to Gaunt and to York. At first, their plight seems to be the same as York's. They dare not open their mouths for fear of the re-percussions. That foul injustice has been done to Gaunt and to his son Bolingbroke is without doubt, but they must tread lightly when considering what action to take. The dialogue is written in such a fashion as to emphasize the volume of wrongs which the king has done. One after another of his deeds is catalogued, all those things we have already heard Gaunt and York accuse him of. The reason for the repetition is to indicate just how widespread the discontent with the king is; in addition, it serves as a way of allowing these individual nobles to garner the courage to decide to commit what will be, after all, treasonable acts. They list all the wrongs, then they pause to consider their weight, and Northumberland speaks for them all when he expresses fear at his own thoughts: he "dares not say" what they can do to set things right in England. It is important to realize that there is something conspiratorial about this scene, in that the three nobles are aware of the gravity of the situation. But when they decide at the end to join forces with Bolingbroke's forces, they do so with conviction.

> . . . we shall shake off our slavish yoke,
> Imp out our drooping country's broken wing,
> Redeem from broking pawn the blemish'd crown [and]
> Wipe off the dust that hides our scepter's gilt. . . .
> (291-94)

Note in these words of Northumberland's the reference to Richard's financial dealings ("redeem from broking pawn") and the pun on the word "gilt," which refers to both the golden scepter, the symbol of the crown which has become besmirched by the king's behavior, and to the actual "guilt" which lay on Richard's head, presumably for the murder of Gloucester. The irony is heavy with significance.

ACT II – SCENE 2

Summary

At Windsor Castle, deep in conversation with Bushy, one of the king's favorites, the queen is trying to discover the source of her deep depression. The king has departed for Ireland, and the queen feels that something ominous is about to occur:

> Yet again, methinks
> Some unborn sorrow, ripe in Fortune's womb
> Is coming towards me. . . .
>
> (8-10)

Her "inward soul" persuades her that there is something amiss caus-
ing her anxiety, something more than mere separation from the king,
although that separation is indeed a source of pain to her.

Green hurries onstage as they are talking and proves the queen's
premonition correct by delivering the news that Bolingbroke has
landed with his army in the north of England. York enters then and
laments the fact that he was left by Richard to uphold the royal
forces, to "underprop the land." There is no money left to fight a successful campaign against the rebels, and even if there were, it seems
apparent that the popular figure in the country is *not* the king but his
adversary – Bolingbroke. Adding to the general woe which has
befallen the present company, a messenger enters with the news that
the Duke of York's sister-in-law, the widow of the late Duke of
Gloucester, has died. "God for his mercy! what a tide of woes/ Comes
rushing on this woeful land at once," cries York in despair. He is
thoroughly confused; he is duty-bound (by conscience and kinship)
to defend the nation against the rebels, but his sympathies are with
his nephew Bolingbroke, whom the king has wronged.

The queen and York leave, and Bushy, Bagot, and Green remain
behind to discuss their plans. Bagot decides to go to Ireland and join
the king, while Bushy and Green decide to seek refuge at a sympathetic castle in Bristol. The three of them are convinced that the
Duke of York's chances of repelling the rebels are slim. The task of
defending Richard's crown, Green likens to "numbering sands, and
drinking oceans dry." Convinced that they "may never meet again,"
they exit.

Commentary

The dramatic strategy of this scene is similar to that which
Shakespeare uses elsewhere and which he will bring to its most
perfect execution in *Macbeth*. He builds suspense and tension by
having a figure of some importance in the play, here the queen, articulate her *premonition* of evil things to come, then after a suitable

interval in which another character, Bushy, tries to dissuade her from her gloomy thoughts, he has the news announced that her *intuition* was *correct*; shortly thereafter, woe upon woe is to be visited upon all present. It is interesting to note that in the queen's immediate response to Green's information about the rebel forces that she even uses a form of imagery which Shakespeare will later have Lady Macbeth use to great effect:

> So, Green, thou art the midwife to my woe,
> And Bolingbroke my sorrow's dismal heir;
> Now hath my soul brought forth her prodigy,
> And I, a gasping, new-delivered mother,
> Have woe to woe, sorrow to sorrow, joined.
>
> (62-66)

The image of giving birth in the context of sorrow and political intrigue (birth given to a monster-prodigy) and all as if first conceived in the imagination (the soul brought forth the monster) is of special importance to this play. First, there is the general theme of legitimacy and inheritance to consider: the play is about a deposition and an unlawful succession to the throne, and for all of its consideration of the inadequacy of the king in question, the process shall bring forth *misery* as its *heir*. Another motif, which Shakespeare makes much of in the last acts of the play, is that of the relationship between one's experience of suffering and the imagination. Later, Richard is isolated in his prison cell and will meditate on the "populous" world of his thoughts and how they breed:

> My brain I'll prove the female to my soul,
> My soul the father; and these two beget
> A generation of still-breeding thoughts. . . .
>
> (V.v. 6-8)

After Bushy's advice to "despair not," the queen continues with her theme and uses phrases which relate the current state of sorrow to their immediate causes:

> Who shall hinder me?
> I will despair and be at enmity

> With cozening hope. He is a flatterer,
> A parasite, a keeper-back of death,
> Who would gently dissolve the bands of life,
> Which false hope lingers in extremity.
>
> (67-72)

Hope, she says, is a flatterer and a parasite and keeps even death at bay; she is speaking these lines to the very characters in the play who have been identified (by most of the sympathetic characters) with the flattery and corruption which will drag Richard down to his doom.

When Bushy is first speaking to the queen, before Green enters with the news about the rebels, he also uses language which prepares us for several later scenes in the play when Richard will become more of a central focus. In a later scene, Richard has an important moment in which he asks for a mirror and then, gazing at his image, he meditates publicly on his situation as king and as an ordinary mortal. Here, Bushy uses a metaphor which obliquely prepares us for that important dramatic moment:

> Each substance of a grief hath twenty shadows,
> Which shows like grief itself, but is not so;
> For sorrow's eye, glazed with blinding tears,
> Divides one thing entire to many objects,
> Like perspectives, which rightly gazed upon
> Show nothing but confusion. . . .
>
> (14-19)

Again, the key idea is that there is a difference between what you *think* you perceive and what is *actually* there, and beyond that, there is the natural distortion which a confused emotional state will bring to one's perceptions. Here the idea is graphically expressed in the image of an eye filled with tears through which one's experience is refracted. As this might be true of the queen in this scene, it is also true to a certain extent of Richard in a later scene. There it will be Bolingbroke who comments sarcastically about the difference between true emotion and "shadows." (This idea is one which fascinated Shakespeare throughout his life, perhaps because he was so closely associated with the stage where it is the business of a good actor to convey the *substance* of true emotions through mere *shadows* (acting) of those emotions.) As a concluding note on this idea, consider the following two brief passages:

> Howe'er it be, I cannot but be sad—
> As, though on thinking on no thought I think,
> Makes me with heavy nothing faint and shrink.
>
> (30-32)

This is spoken by Richard's queen in the scene we are discussing. And this is spoken by another of Shakespeare's mentally tortured heroes, Prince Hamlet, speaking of Denmark.

> . . . for there is nothing either good
> Or bad but thinking makes it so. To me it is a prison.
>
> (II.ii. 255-56)

With the announcement of the arrival of the rebel forces and the death of the Duchess of Gloucester, all talk of imaginary worries ceases. It would be foolhardy to ignore the signs of things to come. An important figure in this scene is the Duke of York, for he has lost a sister-in-law and is dissatisfied with the king, yet he has been appointed to be the guardian of the realm in the king's absence. His feelings are divided:

> Both are my kinsmen.
> Th' one is my sovereign, whom both my oath
> And duty bids defend; t' other again
> Is my kinsman, whom the king hath wronged,
> Whom conscience and my kindred bids to right.
>
> (111-15)

His last words of confusion make it absolutely clear that there is no hope of any real resistance to Bolingbroke, but because he is duty-bound, the Duke of York will, for now, fight for the king.

The last moments of the scene are given over to the three representatives of Richard's court still remaining—Bushy, Bagot, and Green. They present a picture of expedience and cowardice, Bagot being the only one who will go to join the king in Ireland. There is no question concerning whether or not they will join the Duke of York in his battle against Bolingbroke's army. These men are like rats, leaving a sinking ship; here, the ship is England, the ship of state.

ACT II – SCENE 3

Summary

Somewhere in Gloucestershire, once more in England, Bolingbroke questions Northumberland about the way to Berkeley. These "high wild hills and rough uneven ways" have exhausted them both. Northumberland replies that Bolingbroke's "fair discourse" and his good conversation have made the journey seem light and easy. Bolingbroke replies graciously that his companion's words have special value for him.

Northumberland's son, Henry Percy, comes onto the scene and pledges his services to Bolingbroke for life. Northumberland and Bolingbroke then discuss the military situation and are soon joined by the forces of Willoughby and Ross, and both men reaffirm their pledge to right the wrongs done to Bolingbroke in his absence. The Lord of Berkeley enters then, bearing a message from the Duke of York. Berkeley addresses Bolingbroke as "My Lord of Hereford," and Berkeley is rebuffed by the rebel leader, who tells Berkeley to address him by his proper title – Lancaster – if he wants an answer.

The Duke of York, unattended, enters next and is greeted formally and respectfully by Bolingbroke, who kneels to him. York, however, will have none of this formality and tells his nephew to

> Grace me no grace, nor uncle me no uncle;
> I am no traitor's uncle, and that word "grace"
> In an ungracious mouth is but profane.
>
> (86-88)

York reminds Henry and his rebels that "in my loyal bosom lies his [King Richard's] power," but Bolingbroke stands firm in his claim that he has every right to be doing what he is doing. He was banished as Hereford, but now that his father is dead, he returns as Lancaster to claim what is his and "to rouse [Richard's] wrongs." He further entreats old York to think of him as a son (". . . methinks in you/ I see old Gaunt alive"). He continues the kinship argument, trying to persuade York that if the situation had been reversed and it was *York* (instead of Gloucester) who had been killed by Richard, that it is certain that old Gaunt would have backed *Aumerle* (York's son).

Northumberland reiterates the point that *all* of them are concerned primarily with righting the wrongs that have been done to Bolingbroke, and Bolingbroke asks York to join them in attacking Bristol Castle, where the "caterpillars of the commonwealth," Bushy, Bagot, and their accomplices, are hiding. York finds the argument to be strong, and he says, "It may be I will go with you. . . . Things past redress are now with me past care."

Commentary

Bushy, Bagot, and Green had the last words in Scene 2, as they prepared to escape to Ireland, in Bagot's case, or to ensconce themselves in Bristol Castle, as Green and Bushy decided to do. By the end of this scene, the forces of Bolingbroke will be preparing to go to Bristol themselves to clear the land of these "caterpillars of the commonwealth." The scene itself is almost melodramatically opposed to the one which precedes it, setting off the forces of good against their evil opponents.

The way in which Bushy, Bagot, and Green disport themselves is in striking contrast to the behavior of the Bolingbroke faction. Even their lines are overdressed, somewhat genteel and effete, in comparison with the speeches of Bolingbroke and his men. For example, the soldiers have been on their feet for some time. They speak of the hard road they have traveled, and the distance they have yet to go, but as befits their heroic status, they do not complain too loudly. Of particular importance here is the implied reason for their forbearance in these hard times. Notice the way, for example, in which Northumberland speaks to Bolingbroke. It is as though Shakespeare wants to prepare us in advance for Bolingbroke's ascent to the throne. Explaining his renewed energy despite the physical hardships, Northumberland claims that the "noble company" of Bolingbroke has been its chief source. This way of speaking about someone is usually closely associated with a *royal* personage; the impression given is that the very presence of royalty—in this case, Bolingbroke—emanates some lifegiving source. When Henry Percy comes onto the scene and tenders his service to Bolingbroke, one almost imagines him bending his knee and pledging himself as one would to a king. With the arrival of Willoughby and Ross, the effect is redoubled: Shakespeare has these various entrances strung out in this way to give the dramatic illusion of great numbers of people supporting the king-to-be. It is as though Bolingbroke will almost *have* to become the new ruler by popular acclaim. Though no admirer of democracy himself, Shakespeare's idea here is that there is a will of the people (albeit the nobility) which might, in some cases, supercede the divine right of kingship.

When Bolingbroke, in mid-sentence, decides to use his new title of Lancaster, we get the feeling that the popular support *might* have had some effect on this leader of men. But at this point, Bolingbroke still feels uneasy about his position, and he is never too actively in pursuit of power, as, for example, Richard III is, in Shakespeare's play of that name. There is a feeling in this scene that circumstances are mounting which are likely to force certain kinds of commitments from the nobility and, specifically, from Bolingbroke. One should be alert to various shades of indecisiveness and commitment in this scene. This element is used as dramatic material throughout the play.

With all of these "royal indications" in mind, imagine the dramatic effect when Bolingbroke kneels to the Duke of York and calls him "my gracious uncle." It is clear that the duke is the king's representative, but it would be unlikely that Bolingbroke would at this point be thereby showing obeisance to the *king*. Bolingbroke is testing both himself and his uncle with the irony and the seriousness of their situation, and the ensuing conversation between the duke and Bolingbroke is quite serious. Treating issues of importance to the country, Bolingbroke argues soundly that he has been wronged, and in so arguing, he uses language that strikes the central theme of rights of inheritance:

> Will you permit that I shall stand condemned,
> A wandering vagabond, my rights and royalties
> Plucked from my arms perforce, and given away
> To upstart unthrifts? . . . I lay my claim
> To my inheritance of free descent.
>
> (119-36)

The last lines of the scene voice the central dilemma in the words of Bolingbroke and York: Bolingbroke speaks of "weeding" the country of what is choking it, and York grapples with his own conscience over what this weeding entails:

> It may be I will go with you, but yet I'll pause,
> For I am loath to break our country's laws.
> Nor friends, nor foes, to me welcome you are.
> Things past redress are now with me past care.
>
> (168-71)

ACT II – SCENE 4

Summary

A short scene closes this act. In a camp in Wales, the Lord of Salisbury is speaking with a Welsh captain and is worried that he has heard "no tidings from the king." The captain is ready to disperse his troops, but is urged by Salisbury to maintain his forces one more day. The captain, however, refuses; he believes the rumor that "the king is dead." Unnatural omens and portents seem to prove the supposition and "our countrymen are gone and fled." Salisbury, likewise, laments Richard's dying glory – "like a shooting star." Symbolically, Salisbury sees the sun set "weeping in the lowly west."

Commentary

This scene serves in place of a stage battle to tell us that Richard's cause has been lost. The language used by Richard's allies is conventional in its reference to the natural elements being somehow in harmony with the momentousness of the occasion. When great men fall, so goes the popular belief, the echoes of that fall are heard in the earth's crust itself. The tradition can be traced back at least to the time of the crucifixion of Christ, at which time earthquakes and natural calamities were witness to the event. Shakespeare, along with his contemporaries, uses this idea fairly frequently; it is an important motif in all of his history plays. Salisbury's comment on the fall of Richard being "like a shooting star" makes reference to the particular image of Richard in the play as someone who does possess, however one may judge it, a kind of style or romantic glory. This is how he is known and how he knows himself. It is also a conventional metaphor for the "tragic" fall from greatness by a heroic or noble figure.

ACT III – SCENE 1

Summary

Here, Bolingbroke makes his first public, political act. Standing before the castle of Bristol, he passes sentence on Bushy and Green. (Bagot went to Ireland.) He gives a long account of the men's wrongs, including the charges that they "misled a prince, a royal king . . . [and] made a divorce between his queen and him." Furthermore, they seized Bolingbroke's lands, ruined his parks, and removed the coat of arms from his property and, finally, they unjustly urged Bolingbroke's exile. Bolingbroke has had to live in a land not his own, where he "sighed [his] English breath in foreign clouds,/ Eating the bitter bread of banishment." Bolingbroke has not proclaimed himself king, but his actions are very much like those of a king, and the lords present all recognize his authority. He orders the execution of Bushy and Green forthwith. But before the two men allow themselves to be led proudly away, believing their cause to be just, Bushy defiantly proclaims that "more welcome is the stroke of death to me/ Than Bolingbroke to England." Green adds that he is confidant that "heaven will take our souls."

Bolingbroke then turns to the Duke of York and asks him to see that the queen is looked after and kindly commended. York assures him that he has already dispatched a messenger to her. Bolingbroke then announces that he will set out for Wales, where the king has joined Glendower.

Commentary

In order for Bolingbroke's character to assume sufficient dramatic stature, he must be seen to grow into the role of king. Although the entire play is not devoted to the "education of a king," as it is in Shakespeare's *Henry IV, Part I*, it is an important element here for the proper sympathies must be aroused. Two simple things, therefore, take place in this scene, both involving Bolingbroke in something of a public role. We first see him as a dispenser of justice, and it is right that we discern some righteous indignation in his manner of dispatching Bushy and Green. He has good cause to be angered by these corrupters of the king. Note that this is where the emphasis is – on the *tempters* and not on the *tempted*. In *Henry IV, Part I.*, Shakespeare returns to this idea in much more complex form. The play involves some of the same characters as this one. Bolingbroke is there the aging King Henry IV, and it is his son, Prince Hal, who must learn to be the next king. The great worry of King Henry is that his son is being led astray by the low company he is keeping, chief among them being Jack Falstaff.

As benefits the good ruler, the last item which Bolingbroke attends to shows him to be a compassionate man: "For God's sake, fairly let her be entreated," he instructs his companions regarding the queen. He can dispense harsh justice when necessary, but he also has an expansive heart. Compare Bolingbroke's behavior here with the cunning of Richard's public dealings earlier in the play. Shakespeare is writing some rather effective propaganda for Henry Bolingbroke and his successors.

ACT III – SCENE 2

Summary

Bolingbroke was right; Richard has indeed landed back in Wales and is now at Carlisle with his army. He is joyous to be back in his native country again, especially after a difficult crossing of the Irish Sea. He weeps for joy and is convinced that his presence will be enough to deter the rebel forces. In a highly emotional soliloquy, he declares,

> Dear earth, I do salute thee with my hand,
> Though rebels wound thee with their horses' hoofs.
> As a long-parted mother with her child
> Plays fondly with her tears and smiles in meeting,
> So, weeping, smiling, greet I thee, my earth,
> And do thee favours with my royal hands.
>
> (6-11)

He bids the land itself rear up and attack Bolingbroke and his men, but the Bishop of Carlisle wisely suggests that they do something more practical than prattle. "The Power that made you king," he says, will "keep you king in spite of all"; he admonishes that "the *means* that heavens yield must be embraced/ And not neglected" (emphasis mine). Aumerle, York's son, agrees "that we are too remiss/ Whilst Bolingbroke, through our security/ Grows strong and great in substance and in power." Richard does not catch their meaning, however, and reiterates his faith that "The breath of worldly men cannot depose/ The deputy elected by the Lord."

Salisbury enters with the bad news that the Welsh army, believing that the king was slain, disbanded. He says that Richard stayed too long in Ireland; had he returned only a day earlier, Salisbury could have brought him an army of twelve thousand Welshmen. Hearing this, the king falls into despair. "Time hath set a blot upon my pride," he moans; Aumerle turns and reminds him that he should carry himself like a king. Recovering his poise, Richard proclaims confidence in York: the crown *will* be preserved.

Scroop, a loyal follower of Richard, comes on the scene with yet worse news. He announces that the entire British nation, including women, old men, beardless boys, and clergymen have risen up in arms against the king. He also tells the king that Bushy and Green have made their peace with Bolingbroke, but before he can explain what he means, Richard launches into an attack on his fickle friends. (Of course, what actually happened was that those who were captured were executed, but Scroop is unable to reveal this to the king until Richard's tirade is over.)

Aumerle asks a very practical question: "Where is the Duke my father?" York, remember, had been left in charge of the kingdom. The king ignores Aumerle, however, and launches into an extended monologue about the sad fate of kings in this transitory world.

> For God's sake, let us sit upon the ground
> And tell sad stories of the death of kings. . . .
>
> (155-56)

Carlisle then begs Richard not to be so morbidly self-absorbed, but to put his fear of the foe to good use in opposing him. Richard accepts this chiding and says that he has already taken control of himself: "This ague fit of fear is over-blown/ An easy task it is to win our own." Richard's mood, however, is reversed when Scroop continues his report with the information that the Duke of York has joined the rebels who are backing Bolingbroke. Richard plunges once again into despair, and Aumerle is unsuccessful in coaxing him out of it. As the scene ends, Richard says darkly that he will go to "Flint Castle; there I'll pine away." He orders his officers to send their troops home.

Commentary

Richard has been absent from the stage for quite some time by the beginning of this scene so it is necessary for Shakespeare to use bold strokes in re-establishing the character of the king. The number of times which Richard vacillates in his mood and apparently changes his mind in this scene is a clear indication that he is *not* what one would conventionally think of as a solid and inspiring leader. Throughout, he is cajoled and rather babied by his companions. There is sorely lacking in him a sense of manly resolve and rightness.

His first long speech seems promising, however; it is patriotic and rather cock-sure, but too often Richard is fond of "poeticizing." There is something slightly absurd in his entreaty to the *elements* to do his fighting for him. "But let thy spiders," he tells his England, "that suck up thy venom,/ And heavy-gaited toads lie in their way,/ Doing annoyance to the treacherous feet/ Which with usurping steps do trample thee;/ Yield stinging nettles to mine enemies. . . ." The king is supposed to be divine, according to conventional wisdom, but he is also meant to be a natural warrior and a leader. The problem with this theory is that the mortal king who fills the role isn't always up to the standard of the idea, and here, Shakespeare does seem to be indicating the weakness of this theory.

The other men around Richard are good, strong soldiers and are ill at ease when their sovereign indulges in his romantic ecstasies. This is especially clear as the scene progresses, and they must repeatedly insist that he stop acting the weakling.

This would be very simple characterization indeed if it weren't for the fact that Shakespeare gives to Richard, here and elsewhere, such grand lines of poetry that it is difficult to dismiss him as "just" a whining incompetent. This man, who is also a king, deeply feels his *inadequacy*, and perhaps the *absurdity* of his situation, but, more importantly, he seems to observe himself perform. This, at times, renders him virtually immobile. He seems childishly subject to the passing change in fortunes, exchanging phrases like "Have I not reason to look pale and sad?" for "Awake, thou coward majesty! . . ./ Is not the king's name twenty thousand names?" It is true that he indulges himself and cries his woes aloud, and often the tone seems self-indulgent, but on many occasions, he does reach majestic poetic stature:

> Let's talk of graves, of worms, and epitaphs;
> Make dust our paper and with rainy eyes
> Write sorrow on the bosom of the earth. . . .
> For God's sake, let us sit upon the ground
> And tell sad stories of the death of kings:
> How some have been deposed, some slain in war;
> Some haunted by the ghosts they have deposed,
> Some poisoned by their wives; some sleeping killed;
> All murdered: for within the hollow crown
> That rounds the mortal temples of a king
> Keeps Death his court, and there the antic sits,
> Scoffing at his state and grinning at his pomp,
> Allowing him a breath, a little scene,
> To monarchize. . . .
>
> (145-65)

Richard is guilty of "monarchizing," but, one might say, with *style*. Richard is quick, however, to attack the friends he thinks have turned on him—"O, villains, vipers, damned without redemption"—although when he learns that he has misjudged them and that they have been executed as his allies, he doesn't show the remotest sign of remorse. This leaves a strong impression on us, and most likely such actions do not pass unnoticed by his present associates. Richard's fickleness, they would note, can have dangerous consequences for themselves. This, combined with the almost-certain victory of the armies of Bolingbroke, who have the entire nation in their sympathy, leaves the king a pitiful figure by the end of the scene.

ACT III – SCENE 3

Summary

Bolingbroke's forces have marched the hundred miles from Bristol to Flint Castle on the northeastern coast of Wales when this scene opens. Now Bolingbroke stands before the castle with York,

Northumberland, and their attendants. He has sent Northumberland's son Henry Percy into the castle. When Percy returns, he announces that Richard is inside, along with Aumerle, Lord Salisbury, Scroop, and the Bishop of Carlisle. Bolingbroke instructs his lords to deliver a message to Richard that Henry wishes to speak to him. "On both his knees," he instructs them to tell Richard, he will lay his "arms and power,/ Provided that [his] banishment [be] repealed,/ And lands restored again be freely granted."

First Bolingbroke, and then York, notices Richard on the castle wall, and both of them describe his majesty. Bolingbroke sees "the blushing discontented sun" peeking out from "envious clouds"; York urges Bolingbroke to notice Richard closely. To York, Richard still "looks . . . like a king! Behold his eye,/ As bright as is the eagle's. . . ."

Richard speaks first to Northumberland and upbraids him for not showing the requisite courtesy of bending his knee to the king. He wonders if some act of God has dismissed him from his "stewardship." He further instructs Northumberland to tell Bolingbroke that his very presence on English soil is in defiance of the king's express command, and that it is, therefore, treasonous. He accuses Bolingbroke of instigating "the purple testament" of civil war, and he warns him that "ere the crown he looks for live in peace/ Ten thousand bloody crowns of mothers' sons/ Shall ill become the flower of England's face." Northumberland tries to soothe Richard's ire, and he tells him that it is *not* Bolingbroke's intention to use force in any way: "His coming hither hath no further scope/ Than for his lineal royalties. . . ." Richard answers that "all the number of his fair demands/ Shall be accomplished without contradiction." He then turns to Aumerle in shame and wonders aloud if he should send back a defiant answer to Bolingbroke instead. Aumerle advises him to remain calm, that they would do better to give themselves time to find allies before attempting a fight. Richard then cries out in agony, "O that I were as great/ As is my grief, or lesser than my name!" When he hears that he has a message from Bolingbroke, he begins an extended, self-mocking monologue, stripping himself in words of all the accouterments of his royal household and position of power:

> I'll give my jewels for a set of beads,
> My gorgeous palace for a hermitage,
> My gay apparel for an almsman's gown. . . .
>
> (147-49)

At the end of this heavily ironic speech, he refers to his adversary as "King Bolingbroke," asking "Will his Majesty/ Give Richard leave to live till Richard die?"

Bolingbroke shows deference to the office of king by kneeling before Richard and addressing him as "My gracious Lord." Richard refuses to accept Bolingbroke on bended knee with an offer of obeisance, however, and he bids him rise; he says that he will give him what he wants, adding "Your own is yours, and I am yours, and all." Richard then says that he will ride to London; the kingship, it is understood, will be decided on there.

Commentary

The most striking detail in this scene is the appearance of Richard on the castle walls. There must be something majestic about Richard's entrance for the scene to have any power. That Shakespeare wanted it that way can be seen in the reactions which he ascribes to the first two people who see the king. They both see him in a *glorious* aspect, perhaps seemingly more glorious because he is seen from above and from afar. His position above, high above the others, on the castle wall, says as much as the words he speaks. Notice that he presents a strong position to those below him when he speaks to them as the king, but that he weakens visibly in his indecisive aside to Aumerle towards the end of the scene.

After the strong buildup of Bolingbroke as a natural leader, it comes as somewhat of a reversal to see the king back in a position of power, even if it is largely a symbolic position. But the emphasis here is on the fact that Bolingbroke, unlike Richard, is *not* an ambitious man, and he is still rather awed by the idea of majesty and its present physical manifestation. He remains apart throughout most of this scene, as if to emphasize the fact that he does not feel entirely legitimate in his present role. Remember, it is to be characteristic of Bolingbroke that he feels uneasy about his stewardship of the nation. Thus, it is a stroke of dramatic genius to have him appear hesitant about confronting the king, who has just appeared high on a castle wall. Richard's strong warning that the crown will not rest easily on a usurper's head is not lost on Bolingbroke. This theme of ill-fitting royal garments is one which Shakespeare will use again and again in the great tragedies, especially in *Macbeth*.

In this regard, it is important to note that before Richard makes his appearance, we witness a conversation between the Duke of York and Bolingbroke in which the duke reminds him of the importance of what is about to transpire, and that there was a time when had Bolingbroke dared to act as he now is, the king would have wasted no time in having him executed. Bolingbroke's answer, tellingly, is rather ambiguous:

> York: Take not, good cousin, further than you should,
>   Lest you mis-take: the heavens are over our heads.
> Bolingbroke: I know it, uncle, and oppose not myself
>   Against their will.
>
> (16-19)

"Oppose not myself/ Against their will" is the key phrase here. If Bolingbroke emphasizes "oppose not myself," the meaning would be that he is acting in his own self-interest, as he perhaps has the right to do. But there are other shades of meaning apparent if one pauses between "myself," and "Against their will." In that case, his reply could be taken to mean that the heavens themselves would favor Bolingbroke's cause; all it needs is an emphasis on the "against."

When Richard does appear above, Bolingbroke's confidence obviously seems to weaken. His words express a certain awe before the majesty of the king:

> See, see King Richard doth himself appear,
> As doth the blushing discontented sun
> From out the fiery portal of the east,
> When he perceives the envious clouds are bent
> To dim his glory, and to stain the track
> Of his bright passage to the occident.
>
> (62-67)

The phrase "envious clouds" could, of course, refer to Bolingbroke himself, intentionally on his part or not, but that doesn't remove from the passage itself the feeling that we are in the presence of some glorious being, far above us. Earlier, Gaunt made a similar reference to Richard in a negative sense—as one who would expend himself in a "fierce blaze of riot." Here, coming out of "the fiery portal of the east," the context makes him seem heroic.

In Richard's two long speeches, one finds reason for the awed responses of the spectators. There is an authority and dignity with which he speaks to them at first, upbraiding them for their failure to show proper respect for the office of king. When Richard continues, however, his characteristic self-pity begins to take over. What prevents it from descending into mawkishness is a sarcasm in his tone of voice. When Bolingbroke bends his knee to the king, Richard greets him with the words:

> Fair cousin, you debase your princely knee
> To make the bare earth proud with kissing it.
> Me rather had my heart might feel your love,
> Than my unpleased eye see your courtesy.
> Up, cousin, up; your heart is up, I know,
> Thus high at least, although your knee be low.
>
> (190-95)

Here, stage directions are inserted after "Thus high at least." The actor playing Richard is instructed to point to the crown on his head. Bolingbroke, reminded of who addresses him, is rather tight-lipped during this scene, as he usually is in the presence of the king. Thus his awkwardness in the situation leaves him no option but to allow the king to do the speaking. The king, at the very end of the scene, plays on Bolingbroke's reticence, and more or less *forces* him to give an order:

> *Richard*: . . . Set on towards London, cousin, is it so?
> *Bolingbroke*: Yea, my good Lord.
> *Richard*: Then I must not say no.

ACT III – SCENE 4

Summary

Back in the Duke of York's garden, the queen is waiting for news of her husband, and her two lady attendants are trying to distract her gloom. No matter what they suggest as diversion, though, the queen sighs that it would only remind her that the world is cruel and that her sorrow is too heavy to be lifted. While they are walking and she is weeping, they notice a gardener and his men. The queen decides to spy on them in the hope that they might have something to say about the nation and its problems ("They will talk of state; for everyone doth so. . . .").

The gardener gives elaborate instructions to his apprentices about how to prune and trim the plants which they are working on in order to ensure the proper growth and governance of their garden, to prevent its being choked by weeds, and to save it from being in a state of chaos. The servants speak up and make explicit reference to England being like a garden, and they compare Richard and his followers to weeds which once threatened its health. Bolingbroke is named as the one who has "plucked up" those weeds, "root and all." Bolingbroke, they say,

> Hath seized the wasteful King. O, what pity is it
> That he hath not so trimmed and dressed his land
> As we this garden!
>
> (55-57)

The queen holds her silence as long as she can; then she comes forward and accuses the gardener of being beyond his station in talking of the deposition of a king:

> Dar'st thou, thou little better thing than earth,
> Divine his downfall? . . .
>   Speak, thou wretch.
>
> (77-80)

The gardener defends himself by telling the queen that what he has just said is nothing more than common knowledge; all she needs to do is go to London and she will find things exactly as he has described them. The queen decides to do this and she departs. After she has left, the gardener tells his servants that, "in the remembrance of a weeping queen," he will plant a "bank of rue" where the queen's tears have fallen to the earth.

Commentary

This type of scene in Shakespeare's plays has a very special function: there is something contemplative about it, as if Shakespeare wants the audience to have sufficient time to consider some of the issues – political and individually human – which are at stake. That is not to say that there is no emotion in the scene, for we witness the queen's distraught state of mind and her forced silence while the representatives of the common people discuss the demise of Richard; there is clearly an emotional strain in her bearing and in the delivery of her lines in this scene. Also, it is not to be assumed that the gardeners are without feeling, either to the queen or to the nation's desperate condition. The core of the scene, nevertheless, is the long discourse on the sort of care needed to keep a garden at its most productive, a clear and very common metaphor for the kind of governance necessary to keep the nation functioning at its most productive. There is a definite solemnity with which the gardener gives the instructions:

> Go thou, and like an executioner,
> Cut off the heads of too fast growing sprays,
> That look too lofty in our commonwealth;
> All must be even in our government.
> You thus employed, I will go root away
> The noisome weeds, which without profit suck
> The soil's fertility from wholesome flowers.
>
> (33-39)

The gardener is by no means advocating democracy in any form when he says "all must be even in our government"; he is referring to those members of the nobility who have gained excessive favor with the king and who therefore have too much power. To bring things back to "normal," with the proper hierarchy assuming its natural function, these excessive "weeds" and "caterpillars" (an image already referred to) must be removed. Richard is accused only in that he was wasteful and because he did not aid nature in this political pruning operation. The common people, or at least the artisan class as here represented, are perfectly orthodox in their beliefs, recommendations, and wishes.

> Superfluous branches
> We lop away, that bearing boughs may live;
> Had he done so, himself had borne the crown,
> Which waste of idle hours hath quite thrown down.
>
> (63-66)

This scene began, remember, with the queen's attending ladies trying to divert her with various trifling games and songs, but these delights are ineffectual in her present state. It is interesting that one feature of Richard's reign was his delight in courtly entertainments and glamorous display. Starting this scene with oblique reference to "entertainments," inappropriate entertainments at that, it is a subtle variation on one of the themes of this play. The gardener refers to "some few vanities" that will be the only things to weigh in the balance with Richard against Bolingbroke. The vanities are also references to his frivolous entertainment-filled lifestyle.

When the queen speaks of "old Adam's likeness" in referring to the gardener and later asks "What Eve, what serpent, hath suggested thee/ To make a second fall of cursed man?" she is continuing the religious thread that runs throughout the play. As well as describing England as a garden, Shakespeare has her invoke the idea of the Garden of Eden to make it clear that more is at stake than just the *ordinary* affairs of an *ordinary* man. The very act of pruning the garden, if it involves also pruning the king of his power, is an act against God's divine will. The queen reminds us of this point. The gardener would probably agree, but he is really just a powerless man reporting what has happened. Yet the gardener remains a sympathetic character. Even though he is from a lower order of society, he responds to events very much like old Gaunt and perhaps York in his better moments. At the very end of this scene, it is significant that Shakespeare has the queen curse the gardener – "Pray God the plants thou graft'st may never grow" – but the gardener feels no spite; rather, he feels pity for her. This pity which Shakespeare evokes for the queen acts as a prelude and a cue to our response to her husband when we see him in his fallen state later in the play. The gardener's last words understandably evoke sympathy from us:

> Poor queen! so that thy state might be no worse,
> I would my skill were subject to thy curse.
> Here did she fall a tear; here in this place
> I'll set a bank of rue, sour herb of grace.
> Rue, even for ruth, here shortly shall be seen,
> In the remembrace of a weeping queen.
>
> (103-8)

ACT IV – SCENE 1

Summary

This act has only one scene, and it takes place in London, in Westminster Hall, about forty days after the king's surrender at Flint Castle. It focuses on a meeting in Parliament, held to decide the matter of kingship and also to discuss Bolingbroke's actions, as well as those of Richard and his accomplices. Among those present for the council are Bolingbroke, Aumerle, Northumberland, Percy, the Earls of Fitzwater and Surrey, the Bishop of Carlisle, and the Abbot of Westminster. Bagot, who escaped earlier to Ireland and thereby escaped execution at Bristol, has now been captured and is now being questioned about Richard's actions.

Bolingbroke wants to know, first of all, who is responsible for Gloucester's death. Bagot's answer is immediate; he points to Aumerle, the son of York. Aumerle, he says, once boasted that he could dispose of his uncle Gloucester and, moreover, that not even one hundred thousand crowns would be enough to bribe him to help return Bolingbroke to England; England, indeed, would be "blest" if Bolingbroke were killed. Aumerle, of course, denies the charge, but the Earl of Fitzwater, Henry Percy, and another lord substantiate Bagot's accusations. Aumerle is defended by the Earl of Surrey, but Fitzwater charges Surrey with lying and swears that he heard the banished Mowbray say that it was Aumerle who arranged for Gloucester's assassination.

Mowbray, as it turns out, cannot affirm or deny the charges. The Duke of Carlisle informs the group that Mowbray was killed during a crusade to the Holy Land. The Duke of York enters then and announces that Richard, "with willing soul," has yielded up his "high sceptre" to Bolingbroke. To Bolingbroke, he says, "Long live Henry, fourth of that name." Hardly has Bolingbroke accepted the throne, however, than the Bishop of Carlisle objects: no one but God, he says, can judge Richard. He objects to Richard being tried for "apparent guilt" without even being present. Bolingbroke's "trial" of the king, he says, is a "black, obscene" deed, and he prophesies that if Bolingbroke is crowned king, "the blood of English shall manure the ground,/ And future ages groan for this foul act." The civil wars that follow, he vows, will be worse than the Crucifixion itself. Northumberland interrupts the bishop's tirade and orders him arrested and charged with treason.

When Bolingbroke speaks, he calls for Richard to be brought before them so that he himself can surrender "in common view." When Richard is brought in, he remarks on the many once-friendly faces which are now ready to condemn him; Christ had only one Judas. Yet he tempers his emotion when he hands his crown to Henry. He reminds him of the many "cares" that go with the crown; he then renounces his claim to the throne and wishes Bolingbroke "many years of sunshine days."

Northumberland, not swayed by Richard's poignant words of fatalism and resignation, demands that Richard read aloud the charges against him–"Committed by your person and your followers . . . [so that] men/ May deem that you are worthily deposed." Richard, however, says that his tears prevent him from seeing the list of charges. He sobs that he is nothing–a king of snow, melting before "the sun of Bolingbroke." He asks only to "be gone and trouble you no more." Bolingbroke, therefore, orders him to be taken to the Tower of London; the coronation will be performed on the coming Wednesday, he says as he exits.

Alone with the clergymen, Aumerle proposes a plot to do away with Bolingbroke, and the Abbot of Westminster invites Aumerle to his home for further talk. Together, they will conceive such a plot that will "show us all a merry day."

Commentary

Shakespeare sets up a parallel here with the opening scenes of the play. This simple scene, you should note, comprises the entire fourth act. You will recall that the first words of the play were Richard's: he asked Gaunt to bring forth his son, Bolingbroke, to explain charges of treason that he leveled against Mowbray. The situation has virtually reversed itself by Act IV. Here it is Bolingbroke who is doing the ordering and the judging of the cases. He asks Bagot what he knows about the death of Gloucester, significantly the same issue which preoccupied Richard and the nobles in the first scene of the play. The fact is, Richard was conducting something of a sham inquiry in the earlier scene–that is, he was only trying to keep the facts of the matter under cover while not allowing his nobility to become embroiled in too open a dispute. Bolingbroke accused Mowbray – and justifiably so – of treason, and later we find out that it was indeed Mowbray who had a hand in the assassination of Gloucester. Yet the upshot of that first dispute was the exiling of Bolingbroke and Mowbray – on Richard's orders. Years have passed since then, and it is only after suffering the loss of his father, old Gaunt, and the humiliation of having his property unlawfully seized, that Bolingbroke now finds himself in the position of one who can see the full truth revealed concerning what Richard has done and what kind of a man and a king he truly is. Bolingbroke is a victim of grave injustice. Politically it is important for Bolingbroke to raise this issue of Gloucester again so that it be publicly known that *he* has been wronged – he did not deserve banishment – and that the king and his henchmen have been involved in shady actions which run counter to (Act I, Scene 1, and Act IV, Scene 1) have their the best interests of the nation. Thus, the parallel scenes places in the dramaturgical geometry of the play; the revelations and outcome are significantly different because of the political reality which has changed during the course of the play.

The main accusation in this scene is against Aumerle, York's son, who allegedly had involved himself in the plot against Gloucester. Shakespeare constructs the scene in such a way as to emphasize the heated feelings and potentially anarchic situation of the nobles. Aumerle defends himself against first one, Bagot, and then another, Fitzwater, and then yet another, a nameless lord. The repeated attacks on Aumerle and his challenge to fight all of them for his honor are a graphic representation in miniature of the chaos that has been predicted in the event that the anointed king might be deposed. Surrey and Aumerle are pitted against Fitzwater, Bagot, and a nameless lord.

Bolingbroke is silent through much of this bickering, waiting for the opportunity to quell the stormy atmosphere. This he does by seizing on a detail of Fitzwater's report – "I heard the banished Norfolk [Mowbray] say/ That thou, Aumerle, did'st send two of thy men/ To execute the noble Duke" – and announcing that all previous disputes and challenges are now concealed until the noble Mowbray returns from abroad. Bolingbroke's cleverness as an arbitrator is obvious here. One way of forcing all those present to cease their arguments is to make the outcome of the argument hinge on the words of someone who is absent and who won't be able to return for some time.

The Bishop of Carlisle's report that Mowbray died in Italy after spending some time abroad fighting the "black pagans, Turks, and Saracens" changes the tone yet again. All in the company are made to consider the fact that he is buried on foreign soil; this should bring them back to an awareness of the wrongs done to many nobles like him who were forced into exile by King Richard. With the question of Gloucester's assassin conveniently put aside for the moment, Bolingbroke utters a prayer-like commendation of the late Duke of Norfolk: he also ends the dispute for the time being:

> Sweet Peace conduct his sweet soul to the bosom
> Of good old Abraham! Lords appellants,
> Your differences shall all rest under gage,
> Till we assign you to your days of trial.

(103-6)

The next lines in the text announce Bolingbroke as the new king, Henry IV, but before he can gracefully accept York's bid to ascend the throne, the Bishop of Carlisle delivers a long speech warning of the consequences. Remember, here, that it was York in the earlier scenes who delivered this sort of warning. Here it is someone else, a clergyman, warning Bolingbroke and the rest that what they are doing goes against God's will:

> O, if you raise this house against this house,
> It will the woefullest division prove
> That ever fell upon this cursed earth!
> Prevent it, resist it, let it not be so,
> Lest child, child's children, cry against you "woe!"

(145-49)

The heated exchanges and challenges to armed combat which opened this scene are almost a case in point, proving the credibility of the bishop's prophecy.

This speech is an important one because of where Shakespeare positions it in the play. At this point, we have to wonder how Bolingbroke will respond to it. He is aware of the gravity of consequences, and he is not wholly convinced of the rightness of what he is doing. Remember, he is not characterized as an overly ambitious man. He remains quiet throughout Carlisle's speech, and it is Northumberland who orders the Bishop arrested for treason. Bolingbroke doesn't respond in words to the speech, but his first words after it are firm:

> Fetch hither Richard, that in common view
> He may surrender. . . .

(156-7)

Foremost here, we should note Bolingbroke's attentiveness to the bishop's words.

The second part of this act belongs to Richard, with Bolingbroke staying largely in the background. Now one should profitably think of Richard in three ways: first, as a king, one who is aware of the behavior appropriate to the office; next, as a man who is suffering the humiliation of defeat; and, finally, as an actor, as a performer with an awareness of situations and specific audiences. It is exactly where these three "roles," as it were, overlap, that Shakespeare is at his finest as a dramatist. During Richard's speeches in this act, we should always consider where the "performing" and the "reality" become interchangeable. Since we know that Richard is intensely introspective, we need to be aware of clues in his speeches which suggest that we are hearing the "real" Richard, as well as the one who is "putting on a show" and, finally, the Richard who is aware of himself as such. This is a complicated matter, but one which deserves attention.

When thinking of Richard as an "actor," we should recall the two central props which Richard uses in this scene: the crown itself and a mirror which he asks to have brought on especially for him. These are the props of a practiced performer, and he uses them well.

After the first fifteen lines, in which Richard describes himself as a Christ who has more treacherous "apostles" than Jesus did, he asks to hold the crown. During these fifteen lines, he pointedly reminds everyone present that they have, not too long ago, all responded to him as *king*. In former times, the gathered multitude would utter an "Amen" or a "God save the king" after Richard declared his "God save the king." Here, however, there is no response, and Richard has made his point dramatically: "Will no man say 'Amen,' " he asks sarcastically of the silent nobles.

He takes the crown in his hands and bids Bolingbroke take it from him. They hold the crown on either side, while Richard teases his successor with the moment:

> Give me the crown.
> Here, cousin, seize the crown. Here, cousin,
> On this side my hand, and on that side yours.
> Now is this golden crown like a deep well
> That owes two buckets, filling one another,
> The emptier ever dancing in the air,
> The other down, unseen, and full of water.
> That bucket down and full of tears am I,
> Drinking my griefs, whilst you mount up on high.
>
> (181-90)

Here, Richard holds the crown on one side, with both hands, and Bolingbroke on the other, also with both hands. These two possessors of the crown look at each other in all of their manifestations: one on the way up, the other on the way down; one virtually a king, one virtually an ex-king. Here, one might profitably jot down the ways in which they are alike, the ways in which they are dissimilar, and the ways in which this crown (used in this way) is like a mirror into which each looks into his soul and into the soul of his counterpart.

In cataloguing the process of his deposition, Richard is no doubt forcing his audience of nobles to be clearly aware of what they are doing, and he also seems to be working his way up to an emotional outburst. The formality of the repetition makes the speech seem less spontaneous than some of his outbursts, but it prepares the way for something else in the next speech.

> With mine own tears I wash away my balm,
> With mine own hands I give away my crown,
> With mine own tongue deny my sacred state,
> With mine own breath release all duteous oaths.
> All pomp and majesty I do forswear;
> My manors, rents, revenues I forgo;
> My acts, decrees, and statues I deny.
>
> (207-13)

Here Richard is the king stripping himself of all the trappings of his office. In the next speech, he is an ordinary man who is embarrassed that he is to be forced to read an account of his transgressions in public:

> Must I do so? and must I ravel out
> My weaved-up follies? Gentle Northumberland,
> If thy offences were upon record,
> Would it not shame thee, in so fair a troop
> To read a lecture of them?
>
> (228-32)

When Carlisle was defending the king's divine right of rule in the first part of this scene, he used a word which is associated with the pattern of natural imagery running throughout the play. One thinks of the gardener's speech when Carlisle describes the king as God's "captain, steward, deputy elect,/ Anointed, crowned, *planted* many years" (italics mine). Now that Richard is being forced to step down, he describes himself in relation to Bolingbroke in natural imagery which was conventionally associated with royalty:

> O, that I were a mockery king of snow,
> Standing before the sun of Bolingbroke,
> To melt myself away in water drops!
>
> (260-62)

The command to see his own face in a mirror that he may better contemplate himself is perhaps Richard's greatest historical posture. His language is highly poetical, even at one point reminiscent of the famous "face that launched a thousand ships" speech from Marlowe's popular tragedy *Dr. Faustus*. Richard says:

> Was this face the face
> That every day under his household roof
> Did keep ten thousand men? Was this the face
> That, like the sun, did make beholders wink?
> Is this the face which faced so many follies,
> That was at last outfaced by Bolingbroke?
> A brittle glory shineth in this face;
> As brittle as the glory is the face,
> For there it is, cracked in a hundred shivers.
>
> (281-89)

Just before the last line, stage instructions indicate that the actor playing Richard should fling the mirror to the floor. Clearly, Richard is suffering here, but one wonders if he doesn't relish this opportunity for his self-pitying display. Note Bolingbroke's response to the display and Richard's response to that response: "The shadow of your sorrow hath destroyed/ The shadow of your face," says Bolingbroke, after remaining silent through all of Richard's soliloquy. This is a biting remark, for it accuses Richard of play-acting, dealing with "shadows" and pretence instead of showing real emotion. This remark is the more effective because of Bolingbroke's previous long silence. Notice the clipped few words with which Richard responds to this accusation. He is obviously caught off guard:

> Say that again.
> The shadow of my sorrow! Ha! let's see.
> 'Tis very true, my grief lies all within;
> And these external manners of laments
> Are merely shadows to the unseen grief
> That swells with silence in the tortured soul.
>
> (291-96)

This witty answer comes only after Richard has bought himself time to recover with "Ha! let's see."

The last exchanges between Richard and Bolingbroke are in the form of short sentences. Richard's rhetorical flourishes are at an end; he wants to bring the whole sordid business to a conclusion. His lines are the last ironic gasps of a defeated, once-lordly sovereign:

> *Richard*: Being so great, I have no need to beg.
> *Bolingbroke*: Yet ask.
> *Richard*: And shall I have?
> *Bolingbroke*: You shall.
> *Richard*: Then give me leave to go.
> *Bolingbroke*: Whither?
> *Richard*: Whither you will, so I were from your sights.
>
> (309-15)

Richard puns on the word "conveyors" in his exit line, calling them all thieves who "rise thus nimbly by a true king's fall."

The scene and the act do not end, however, with the exit of the deposed Richard and the man who has just announced his own coronation date. Shakespeare presses the point that civil strife is in the air after the deposition by having the last people on stage act and sound like conspirators. The Abbot of Westminster, the Bishop of Carlisle, and Aumerle remain behind. The Abbot's last line is: "I'll lay/ A plot shall show us all a merry day." The play is not yet over. Richard's spirit of greed and power has infected even a man of the church.

ACT V – SCENE 1

Summary

The last act opens with Richard on his way to the Tower. The queen is onstage, waiting for her husband to pass by so that she may tell him goodbye. When she sees him, she likens him to a "beauteous inn" that houses Grief; she likens Bolingbroke to a "common alehouse." She urges her husband to stand tall; it pains her to see him not only deposed, but physically bowed. She wonders if Bolingbroke has also usurped Richard's intellect, for he seems, truly, a ruined man. Richard begs her not to grieve and urges her to leave England and to enter a convent in France.

Northumberland enters and tells Richard that Bolingbroke has changed his mind: Richard is to go to Pomfret and not to the Tower. The queen, he says, has been ordered to France. Richard turns to Northumberland and compares him to a ladder that Bolingbroke used to ascend to Richard's throne. He warns Northumberland that fear and hate will soon separate him and Bolingbroke. But Northumberland refuses to argue with Richard, and he also refuses to allow the queen to follow her husband to Pomfret or him to follow her to France. With deep sorrow, Richard turns to his wife and pleads that their goodbyes be brief, for they make "woe wanton with this fond delay." They part, then, for the last time.

Commentary

In this scene we see Richard in a close-up portrait with his wife, and the emotional quality of the scene balances that of the one which preceded it. Then, he was a man of display before his former subjects; here he is a private man saying goodbye to his wife. The queen's lines, in which she describes him at the beginning of the scene set the tone. Richard is a man to be pitied, a shadow of his former self, a "withering rose." When she compares him to Bolingbroke, she uses a metaphor which characterizes Richard as something elegant and special, while Bolingbroke is common. There is an irony here, of course, as it is Bolingbroke's very "commonness" which accounts in part for his transition to the throne. Earlier in the play, Richard commented on Bolingbroke's popularity with the common people. This will be picked up again in the *Henry* plays, in which Bolingbroke's son, Hal, is noted for having "the common touch," in the best meaning of the phrase.

A curious thing happens in this scene. Not only does the queen's pity set the tone in general for this scene, but the fact that her pity finally becomes annoyance is also significant. She becomes angered by what seems to her to be Richard's too-easy compliance with his fate. Although it is a piteous sight to gaze on greatness fallen low, to her it is also loathsome to see that former greatness going to its slaughter like a lamb. She uses the conventional symbol of the proud lion to make her point: Richard should act like the king of beasts and continue to struggle to the end. This is not the first time that Shakespeare presents Richard within the framework of this metaphor, but one should resist the temptation to label him too quickly; the author's characterization of Richard is a complex one, and Shakespeare doesn't allow a simple progression of responses to the king.

While we can sympathize with Richard in his private suffering, it is a fact that this private suffering occasionally degenerates into self-pity. It seems as though Richard almost *enjoys* the fantasy of imagining weeping, aged women sitting around a fire during a deep winter's night and telling the woeful and lamentable story of poor King Richard.

With relief, we finally see Richard seem to spring to life during his verbal attack on Northumberland in the next part of the scene. His first two lines, calling Northumberland a mere "ladder" which Bolingbroke used to climb to the throne, opens an attack upon Northumberland and expresses a warning to him and those like him: treason and distrust will breed more of the same, and none of those involved will see a happy end to this business. This is really the first time in the play where Shakespeare has Richard sound this theme so forcefully and explicitly, and Northumberland's easy dismissal of the advice—"My guilt be on my head, and there an end"—betrays a suspiciously cocky and over-confident attitude.

An important point about the conclusion to the scene is the physical action which Shakespeare adds to it. Where it may be difficult to sympathize unqualifiedly with Richard, especially when he is dramatizing his own situation, it is easy to imagine him kissing his wife farewell, then kissing her farewell again, as if to delay the inevitable parting. The farewell is poignant, the tone much like that when Gaunt parted for the last time from Bolingbroke.

> One kiss shall stop our mouths, and dumbly part;
> Thus give I mine, and thus take I thy heart.
>
> (95-96)

ACT V – SCENE 2

Summary

In this scene, two or three months have elapsed since Richard was taken to Pomfret. The Duke of York is telling his wife what has happened – how Richard and Bolingbroke arrived in London, how the crowd "threw dust and rubbish" on Richard's head, and how Bolingbroke was hailed with many welcomes and blessings. He thinks that "Heaven hath a hand in these events," and he says that he has sworn allegiance to Bolingbroke.

York sees his son, Aumerle, approaching and says that not only has Aumerle been reduced in rank but that he himself has made a pledge in Parliament for Aumerle's loyalty to Bolingbroke. When York and his wife speak to their son, Aumerle is clearly out of sorts: he does *not* know who the favorites are at court ("the violets now/ That strew the green lap of the new come spring"), nor does he care, and, furthermore, he tells his father that he does *not* know who's jousting at Oxford. His spirit pales, however, when his father mentions to him a sealed paper which he has spied in Aumerle's pocket. A quarrel ensues, and York seizes the paper and reads it. He loudly denounces his son for being a traitor, and he calls for his boots. Despite his wife's pleas and protestations, he means to reveal what he has learned to Bolingbroke. He and his wife quarrel bitterly over Aumerle's treason. York's wife calls her husband unnatural for disclaiming their son, and he calls her a fool for her blind love. After York leaves, his wife pleads with Aumerle to get to the king before York does. Meanwhile, she herself will saddle up and try to delay

York: "Never will I rise up from the ground/ Till Bolingbroke have pardon'd thee."

Commentary

There is something oddly farcical about this scene in an otherwise humorless play: we get a glimpse into the household of one of the minors actors in the political drama where the strife of the outside arena is seen in miniature.

Earlier, York was a defender of Richard and the divine right of kingship. When the situation became intolerable, he switched his allegiance to Bolingbroke. This was an important switch because it was not done capriciously. York had difficulty in coming to his decision, and although one might be tempted to see York as a political time-server, it doesn't seem that Shakespeare wanted him to be judged too harshly. York's heart seems to be in the right place, and the interests of the nation at large seem to have motivated him to do what he did. In this scene, we see that his son, Aumerle, has remained faithful to the previous ruler. Why not? His father's sympathies had been there too at one time. Aumerle's personal loyalty supercedes his questionable duty to the new king. Questionable, in fact, is the only word we can use concerning loyalty in this case, because one must remember the new king's legitimacy as a monarch is in doubt.

The struggle between the father and son seems serious enough, because finally Aumerle's mother has to break in and try to make her husband leave the matter alone and put all thoughts of their turning their only child over to the authorities completely out of his head. They struggle over his boots, most likely (this is not completely clear from the text); she tries to keep them from him, and he tries to put them on so that he can ride to inform Bolingbroke of the plot against his life. Her lines are those of a distracted mother: "Strike him, Aumerle. Poor boy, thou art amazed." His are those of a perhaps over-zealous patriot: ". . . were he twenty times my son,/ I would appeach him."

The purpose of this scene is twofold: first, it shows the results of the political uncertainty and impending chaos at the local level, where most ordinary humans would experience it. (A family spat is a civil war in miniature.) And second, it presents the odd games which fortune plays with political loyalties and political necessities. Who is correct in his loyalty? The father's loyalty to the newly crowned king, or the son's loyalty to the man whom he has served? Shakespeare raises the question without answering it. Aumerle's part in the plot and the outcome of his mother's appeal will feature importantly in the next scene.

One final note on this scene should be made concerning the description of Richard, again the performer. This is important as a prelude to Richard's final scene and his now-famous soliloquy. York describes him thus:

> As in a theatre, the eyes of men,
> After a well-graced actor leaves the stage,
> Are idly bent on him that enters next,
> Thinking his prattle to be tedious;
> Even so, or with much more contempt, men's eyes
> Did scowl on gentle Richard.

> (23-28)

One thing this speech does is identify Bolingbroke as the next "actor" in the role of king. The two men gazed into each other's faces through the hollow crown in an earlier scene; we shall see that in more ways than one they will prove to be "mirror images" of one another.

ACT V – SCENE 3

Summary

Bolingbroke, now Henry IV, laments to Henry Percy that Prince Hal, the heir to the throne, is wasting his life with dissolute companions, and that it has been "full three months since I did see him last."

Aumerle suddenly rushes on stage and asks for a private audience with the king, and when it is granted, he proceeds to beg forgiveness for his involvement in an assassination plot against the crown. With the door locked, Aumerle is prepared to confess, but before he does so, the Duke of York comes to the door and demands that the king should beware of the traitor in his midst. The door is opened, and York dashes in and loudly accuses his son.

"O heinous, strong and bold conspiracy!" shouts Bolingbroke, "O loyal father of a treacherous son." Before any action can be taken, however, the Duchess of York arrives and begs forgiveness of the

king in behalf of her son. The king throws up his arms and responds
.to the turn of events by saying that

> Our scene is altered from a serious thing,
> And now changed to "The Beggar and the King"
> (79-80)

The duke and duchess then revive the family squabble of the previous
scene and fall on each other in front of the king; they all kneel, making
their various pleas, until the king silences them with his decisive judgment: "I pardon him, as God shall pardon me." Bolingbroke then
declares that he will execute all of the other conspirators. Quietly, the
duchess takes her son in hand and they leave the stage. She vows to
Aumerle that she will pray until "God make thee new."

Commentary

Bolingbroke is now the leader of the nation. What does that
mean? For one thing, as Richard predicted, he will never be fully
secure for the rest of his days. There is a conspiracy afoot, the first of
many, one supposes. And, to make matters worse, as is brought out
in the first part of the scene, the king has an unregenerate son, Prince
Hal, who whiles away his time with Jack Falstaff (particularly in the
Henry IV plays of the tetralogy).

Another errant son, York's, breaks onto the scene as the agent of
the conspiracy. One must imagine Bolingbroke taking the threat
when it is revealed to him by York, quite seriously. There is a real
danger to the throne. But when the duchess enters the scene, a bit of
the farce of the previous scene spills over into this one. Bolingbroke
is now involved in a petty domestic dispute, or what seems like such.
There is a pronounced difference between the glamour associated
with rulers and ruling and between the tedious reality of this sort of
administration and arbitration on a daily basis. This does seem to be
Shakespeare's point, or at least one of them, because this scene is in
such marked contrast with the rather philosophical heaviness of the
entire play up until now. Our last view of Richard was a philosophical one; Shakespeare focused primarily on the idea of kingship and
what it was. Here, the reality is exposed, with all its boring,
melodramatic features. Richard was aloof. That was one reason for
his downfall. Henry is *not* aloof; for that reason, one can easily

imagine (from this scene) the price which he will pay for keeping himself caught up in petty embroilments.

The vehemence with which York denounces his son seems odd, as if Shakespeare wanted to discredit an over-zealous patriotism. York's words, echoing the theme of civil strife, are harsh:

> If thou do pardon, whosoever pray,
> More sins for this forgiveness prosper may.
> This festered joint cut off, the rest rest sound;
> This let alone will all the rest confound.
>
> (83-86)

The wisdom is politically sound perhaps, but in reference to his own son, it is certainly extreme. Bolingbroke pardons the son as an act of mercy, showing himself the good ruler in this, but he also despatches the other conspirators without hesitation: "Destruction straight shall dog them at the heels." He seems to believe firmly in justice and mercy—as a good ruler must—and Shakespeare *did* want to show him as a good ruler.

ACT V–SCENE 4

Summary

This short scene, consisting of only eleven lines, takes place a few months later. In Windsor Castle, Sir Pierce of Exton is speaking to his servant; he interprets Bolingbroke's words "Have I no friend will rid me of this living fear" to mean that Bolingbroke wants someone to kill Richard and put an end to all thoughts of a counter-coup in the country. He explains to his servant that Bolingbroke uttered these words twice—and looked at Exton "as [if he would] say, 'I would thou wert the man. . . .'" Exton's servant confirms Bolingbroke's words and his actions. Exton says finally, "Come, let's go./ I am the King's friend, and will rid his foe."

Commentary

This scene's action is short and straightforward: Sir Pierce Exton interprets Bolingbroke's words "Have I no friend will rid me of this living fear" to mean that he wants someone to kill Richard and put an end to all thoughts of a counter-coup in the country. He explains this to another man and they go to kill Richard. Because of this information, our reception of Richard's final soliloquy will be that much more acute.

ACT V – SCENE 5

Summary

The scene opens as Richard is sitting alone in his cell at Pomfret Castle. His only companions, he says, are his thoughts. Thus he speaks aloud. He "peoples" the world with his thoughts and "plays in one person many people" in his imagination. When he hears music from outside his prison cell, it disturbs him: "How sour sweet music is/ When time is broke, and no proportion kept." The music maddens him, for the giving of this music to him is a sign of love in the giver, and, to Richard, love "is a strange brooch in this all-hating world."

His soliloquy – in which he compares himself with a clock measuring time, his thoughts being the minutes, his eyes being the dials, and his groans being the striking of the hours – is interrupted when a groom, one of his former servants, enters. The groom remembers having tended to Richard's horse during happier days, and he would like to talk to his former king, but Richard becomes irritated when he hears that Bolingbroke now rides proudly on Richard's "roan Barbary." Richard curses his horse, then speaks words of forgiveness.

A keeper breaks off their conversation and offers Richard his meal. Richard, however, says that he won't eat until the food is first tasted by the guard; he is afraid of being poisoned. The keeper says that Sir Pierce of Exton "commands the contrary."

Exton enters with henchmen and a fight breaks out. After killing one of the would-be assassins, Richard is killed by Exton, but before he dies, he curses his killer:

> That hand shall burn in never-quenching fire
> That staggers thus my person.

(109-10)

Richard's dying words affect Exton; "O would the deed were good!" he says. Clearly he fears the consequences of what he has done.

Commentary

Here we see Richard at his most naked and honest. His thoughts, he says, could fill this little world in place of people. During his reign, he needed people as audiences and companions; this explains the flatterers in his court, those who contributed to his downfall. But even the world of thoughts, like the world of people, has a falling out with itself: there is not one *single* thought that enters his head that cannot be immediately countered with its contrary. Even the Bible is not immune to this fact of contradiction. "Come, little ones," says the word of God, but the same book also says that it is as hard to "come," as it is for a camel to pass through the eye of a needle. The association between contrary thoughts, opposing ideas, and the topsy-turvy turn of events in England and in Richard's life is apparent here:

> Thoughts tending to content flatter themselves
> That they are not the first of fortune's slaves,
> Nor shall not be the last; like silly beggars
> Who, sitting in the stocks, refuge their shame,
> That many have and others must sit there;
> And in this thought they find a kind of ease,
> Bearing their own misfortunes on the back
> Of such as have before endured the like.

> (23-30)

Optimistic or rationalizing thoughts, then, are false flatterers to themselves and serve no useful purpose in the end. Richard recapitulates his experiences succinctly: "Thus play I in one person many people." He has played many people and many roles throughout the course of this play, and now in his imagination, he re-runs the gamut of the types. He has played the king, and he quakes from fear of treason; he has played the beggar, and he feels crushed by penury into thinking he was better off as king. The end result of this "logic" is that he *would* be better off dead:

> But whate'er I be,
> Nor I, nor any man that but man is,

> With nothing shall be pleased, till he be eased
> With being nothing.
>
> (38-41)

The chords of music heard from outside the cell have a marked effect on Richard. This scene is the most contemplative in the play, and its "philosophy" speaks of a different kind of concern to Shakespeare in this part of the play from what has gone before. Compare the tone of this scene with the "petty squabbling" found in the two preceding ones. In evoking this difference, the music serves the function of being a mood setter. As an art form, music seems able to "articulate" things which cannot be expressed in any other way. Richard's melancholy is thus underscored. Also, the perfect measure and construction of the phrases of music jar on Richard's ear because it unhappily reminds him of his own discordant state of mind:

> And here have I the daintiness of ear
> To check time broke in a disordered string;
> But for the concord of my state and time
> Had not an ear to hear my true time broke.
> I wasted time, and now doth Time waste me.
>
> (45-49)

The play on words—"time" in music, in the sense of measured duration, and "Father Time"—leads to Richard's observation on his own demise:

> So sighs, and tears, and groans
> Show minutes, times, and hours. . . .
>
> (57-58)

At the end of the speech, Richard seems to grow energetic in his anger, shouting, "This music mads me." As he is not so predisposed, music cannot exercise its calming effect on him.

Shakespeare presents the interlude with the groom as a way of reminding Richard of former, better times, and therefore redoubling the pain of his present state. The groom also serves to show that among some of the common people, there is still respect and feeling for Richard. In addition, the groom has secret thoughts which are perhaps rebellious in nature: "What my tongue dares not, that my heart shall say."

To impress us with the villainy of murdering the king, Shakespeare has Exton recoil in horror from his own accomplishment:

> As full of valor as of royal blood!
> Both have I spilled. O, would the deed were good!
> For now the devil that told me I did well
> Says that his deed is chronicled in hell.
>
> (114-17)

The tradition that regicide originates in hell is here repeated.

ACT V – SCENE 6

Summary

Some days after Richard has been killed, Bolingbroke is talking with York, and he tells him that rebel forces "have consumed with fire" a town in Gloucestershire, and it cannot be ascertained whether or not the rebels themselves have been killed or captured. But there is good news, for Northumberland announces that "the heads of Salisbury, Spencer, Blunt, and Kent" have been sent to London. It is next Fitzwater's turn to speak: "The heads of Brocas and Sir Bennet Seely," men who were involved in the Oxford plot to kill Bolingbroke, have also been sent to London. Henry Percy enters then and tells them that the "grand conspirator," the Abbot of Westminster, "hath yielded up his body to the grave," and that Carlisle is being brought as a captive before them. The king sentences Carlisle to life imprisonment; he spares his life because of the "high sparks of honor in thee have I seen."

Exton enters then and presents Richard, lying in his coffin, to Bolingbroke and is rebuked by the king. Exton declares that he killed Richard because of Bolingbroke's own words, but Bolingbroke is deaf to these excuses. He banishes Exton and vows to "make a voyage to the Holy Land" to expiate the guilt which he has accrued to himself.

Commentary

This last scene of the play swells with details of civil horror: a razed town, six beheadings, one life imprisonment, one banishment, and the corpse of a murdered king. The prophecies of doom seem to be fulfilling themselves. Bolingbroke thanks "gentle Percy" for his part in fighting the rebels. (In *Henry IV, Part I*, Shakespeare shows Henry Bolingbroke's armies in pitched battle against this same Percy.) The mercy which Bolingbroke shows Carlisle, in sparing his life, attests to the general misery of the scene momentarily, but no sooner is the sentence of life imprisonment offered, than Exton arrives with Richard's coffin. The note of damnation and possible regeneration through penance which Bolingbroke's last speech contains concludes the play in the religious imagery which has been threaded throughout.

SIXTEENTH-CENTURY POLITICAL THEORY

Since *Richard II* and the *Henry IV* plays are basically political ones, it is necessary to understand the political doctrine behind them if one is to do justice to Shakespeare's intentions. Elizabeth I, the fifth Tudor to rule England, had come to a throne which was in many ways insecure because of rival claims. Henry VIII, her father, had found it especially necessary to inculcate the doctrine of absolute obedience to the Crown after the break with Rome in 1536. During his reign he had experienced the Pilgrimage of Grace, a rebellion in northern England, and, later, the Exeter Conspiracy, an alleged attempt to depose Henry and place a Yorkist on the throne of England. After Henry VIII's death, England endured the Western Rebellion of 1549; during Elizabeth's reign there occurred the Rebellion of 1569, as well as plots against the queen's life, notably the Babington Plot, which led to the trial, conviction, and execution of Mary, Queen of Scots. Throughout the century and beyond, England had reason to fear an invasion and the uprising of native Catholics. The danger was by no means restricted to the year 1588, when Philip II of Spain sent his Armada to subdue England.

In view of such challenges to Tudor supremacy, there was a need for a political philosophy which would prevent challenges to royal authority and prevent devastating civil war. The basic arguments were developed during the reign of Henry VIII and augmented as new crises arose during the reigns of Edward VI and Elizabeth I. It found expression in officially approved pamphlets and tracts, and also in drama and non-dramatic poetry. Especially it was emphasized in official sermons, the first group of which was introduced in the year

1549. These included strongly worded instructions on the subject of obedience. They were augmented in 1570, following the Rebellion of 1569 and the papal decree of excommunication of Queen Elizabeth I. Every Englishman was required to hear the sermons on obedience three times during the year. The gist of the doctrine was this: the ruler was God's lieutenant on earth; no subject, however exalted, had the right to actively oppose him. To do so was a sin against religion, punishable by suffering here and now and by eternal damnation after death. Even if the ruler were a tyrant, the subject had no right to oppose him; for the head of state ruled with God's sufferance. In support of this doctrine, appeals were made primarily to biblical authority. Texts such as Romans 13 and Proverbs 8, as well as ones in Matthew, were cited repeatedly. John of Gaunt, Duke of Lancaster, summed up the doctrine accurately and concisely in his response to his sister-in-law, the Duchess of Gloucester, who reminded him that the reigning king, Richard II, had been responsible for the death of her husband and Gaunt's brother:

> God's is the quarrel, for God's substitute,
> His deputy anointed in His sight,
> Hath caus'd his death; the which if wrongfully,
> Let Heaven revenge; for I may never lift
> An angry arm against His minister.
>
> (I.ii.37-41)

That Henry IV should so suffer is to be explained by the fact that he, son of John of Gaunt, did "lift an angry arm against [God's] minister." He endures rebellion; he sees the apparent waywardness of Prince Hal as part of his punishment; he is not permitted to lead a crusade against the foes of Christianity and do penance for his grievous sins. But, according to Tudor political theory, he wore the crown by God's authority; no subject had the right to oppose him. All this should make understandable the Percys' position and make unacceptable the view that Henry IV is a hypocrite.

CHARACTER SUMMATIONS

Richard II

As a king, Richard is supposedly divine and all powerful; as a man, he is an ordinary mortal and prey to his own weaknesses. The private tragedy of the play, for Richard, is in his being forced to face this duality. Shakespeare demonstrates that Richard is perhaps temperamentally not fit for the role which history would have him play. His decisions as a monarch seem irrational and arbitrary; he won't listen to the sane advice of old Gaunt, and he insensitively seizes wealth belonging to his noblemen.

It is only during his deposition and his imprisonment that Richard shows his greatest strength as a dramatic figure. Although occasionally he seems to demonstrate self-pity (Bolingbroke accuses him of this), he also reveals himself to have an acute awareness of the ironies and absurdities in the structure of power in his kingdom. Although he keeps reminding those present of his God-given mandate to rule, he seems also to take pleasure in passing on the trials of kingship to his successor.

Richard's last speeches are among the most beautiful in the play. It is as though Shakespeare were allowing the man himself, stripped of political power, a chance to achieve a human power which surpasses suffering and becomes self-knowledge.

Henry Bolingbroke

Bolingbroke contrasts with Richard in many ways. He seems practical minded, honest, and sensitive – in many ways, the "natural" king. It is also important to realize that in the early stages of the play Bolingbroke is, at best, a reluctant rebel. The insult to himself and his father and the urging which he receives from his peers are the determining factors in his effort to depose Richard. He is keenly aware of the magnitude of the crime which he is embarking on, and he quickly learns the tediousness of being a ruler, as is particularly evident in the scene which precedes Richard's prison cell monologue. Whereas Richard's tragic situation catapults his speech into a kind of poetry, Henry's newly placed crown lowers him down into the center of a domestic squabble. His last decision, to make a pilgrimage to the Holy Land, underscores his uneasiness with his new role as king.

John of Gaunt

Bolingbroke's father serves as a kind of spiritual touchstone for the play. Near death, he is impatient with the prevarications of the king and his courtiers; he accuses them of undermining the solid state of England. His rousing patriotic speeches put the political theme of the play directly before the audience. When Richard insults old Gaunt, it is tantamount to sacrilege and treason. When Richard, in effect, steals Gaunt's wealth after his death, it gives Henry Bolingbroke more than enough personal reason for rebelling against the king.

The Duke of York and Aumerle

York and Gaunt should be thought of together. Both seem to represent solid qualities in the English character. It is significant that York struggles with his own sense of what is orthodox and right before throwing in his lot with the rebels. Like old Gaunt, York has a son, but whereas Bolingbroke is the one to depose the king, York's son Aumerle remains loyal to Richard. The father and son are at each other's throats before the end of the play over the question of loyalty to the present ruler. Bolingbroke forgives Aumerle of his possible treachery, but the point is made that the political struggle has repercussions—even down to the ordinary family level.

QUESTIONS FOR REVIEW

1. How do the political themes and private themes in the play interconnect?

2. In what ways can Richard be considered a tragic figure?

3. Discuss the imagery of gardens and gardening in the play.

4. Contrast Richard and Henry as rulers.

5. Is this play humorless?

6. How do the minor characters such as Mowbray, Aumerle, Bushy, Bagot, and Green function in the play?

7. What is the particular function of the women in this play?

8. To what extent does the death of Gloucester affect Richard's deposition?

9. Defend York's change of allegiance to Bolingbroke.

10. Richard is often said to be an "unkingly" ruler. Discuss.

SELECTED BIBLIOGRAPHY

ADAMS, J. Q. *A Life of William Shakespeare.* Boston: Houghton Mifflin Co., 1923.

ALEXANDER, PETER. *Shakespeare.* Oxford: Oxford University Press, 1964.

BEVINGTON, DAVID. *Shakespeare.* Arlington Heights, Ill.: A.H.M. Publications, 1978.

BLOOM, EDWARD A., ed. *Shakespeare 1564-1964.* Providence: Brown University Press, 1964.

BRADLEY, A. C. *Shakespearean Tragedy.* London: The Macmillan Co., 1904.

CHARLTON, H. B. *Shakespearean Tragedy.* Cambridge, England: Cambridge University Press, 1948.

CRAIG, HARDIN. "The Great Trio," *An Interpretation of Shakespeare.* Columbia, Missouri: Lucas Brothers, 1966.

FARNHAM, WILLARD. *The Medieval Heritage of Elizabethan Tragedy.* Berkeley, California: University of California Press, 1936.

GIBSON, H. N. *The Shakespeare Claimants.* New York: Barnes & Noble, Inc., 1962.

HEILMAN, ROBERT B. *Magic in the Web.* Lexington, Kentucky: University of Kentucky Press, 1956.

KNIGHT, G. WILSON. *The Wheel of Fire.* London: Oxford University Press, 1930.

LEAVIS, F. R. *The Common Pursuit.* Hardmonsworth, Middlesex: Penguin Books, Ltd., 1963.

RIBNER, IRVING. *Patterns in Shakespearean Tragedy.* New York: Barnes & Noble, Inc., 1960.

SEWELL, ARTHUR. *Character and Society in Shakespeare.* Oxford: Clarendon Press, 1951.

SPIVACK, BERNARD. *Shakespeare and the Allegory of Evil.* New York: Columbia University Press, 1958.

STIRLING, BRENTS. *Unity in Shakespearean Tragedy: The Interplay of Theme and Character.* New York: Columbia University Press, 1956.

NOTES

NOTES

NOTES